DATE			

LACANDON ADVENTURE
(Last of the Mayas)

Also by the author:
Tarahumara Indians

LACANDON ADVENTURE
(Last of the Mayas)
by Jonathon F. Cassel

Line Drawings and Photographs
by Jonathon F. Cassel, Jr.

The Naylor Company
Book Publishers of the Southwest
San Antonio, Texas

Library of Congress Cataloging in Publication Data

Cassel, Jonathon F
    Lacandon adventure: the last of the Mayas.

    1. Lacandon Indians. I. Title.
F1221.L2C37   970.3   74-18403
ISBN 0-8111-0557-1

Dedication

To my wife Estelle, and son Jon, whose love, devotion, and rare willingness to go anywhere my interests may lead and share the hardships and danger with me, numbers me among the most fortunate of men.

List of Illustrations

viii

Introduction

The state of Chiapas, Mexico, borders on the Pacific Ocean, and the western land frontier of Guatemala. It is the southernmost, and perhaps the least generally known area within the republic. The western geographical sector of Chiapas is composed of incredibly beautiful and extremely rugged mountains. Beyond the Sierras a vast lowland wilderness stretches eastward to the Guatemala boundary. This wild region is known as the "Selva Lacandon."

During the monsoon season which extends from May through December, the selva, or jungle, is subjected to a total rainfall in excess of 100 inches. The superabundant rains have created a multigreen umbrella of dense forests, and wide expanses of jungle so matted with trees and vegetation the sunlight cannot penetrate to the dank and rotting floor.

Deep and treacherous rivers snake their way through the jungles on escape routes to the freedom of the Gulf of Mexico. Foremost of these waterways are the mighty Usamacinta, the Lacanja, the Jatate, and the Lacantun. Throughout the region many turquoise blue lakes lie in shimmering isolation.

The jungle churns with life. Brilliantly plumed birds of many species lace the dark shadows with lilting song, mingled with bursts of raucous discord. Hungry hordes of mosquitos, flies, gnats, and other biting insects hum, whine, and buzz as they incessantly search for warm-blooded victims. Deadly serpents patiently lie in wait for unwary prey, and carnivorous animals engage in hide-and-seek — a never-ending contest of survival or death. Howler monkeys cling to liana vines and rend the air with hair-raising imitations of the jaguar's fearsome roar. All the while, that magnificent beast prowls his domain on padded feet, unafraid, yet feared by all.

This savage, unyielding environment is the homeland of the nearly extinct Lacandon Indians, considered to be the purest descendants of the great Maya civilization that suddenly and mysteriously disappeared during the tenth century, A.D.

During the Spanish reign of terror and conquest, the Lacandons were a strong, warrior tribe who fiercely resisted many efforts by the white invaders to subdue them. One of the major and decisive engagements was fought at a site lying east of where now stands the city of Comitan.

History records that a river flowing through the battle area "ran red with the blood of both sides," so vicious was the fighting. The gun and sword of the mighty Spaniards were no match against the primitive bow and arrow of the jungle-bred Lacandon warriors. The intruders were soundly defeated. To this day the proud and unbending Lacandons have remained an unconquered people.

Except for an unknown number of individuals isolated from the main groups either by choice, or tribal exile, the Lacandons live in three widely separated settlements, or villages. An accurate census would be difficult to obtain. According to government estimates, there are probably less than 150 Lacandons in existence.

One of the Lacandon settlements is located at Lacanja, near the famous Mayan ruins of Bonampak. Another is at Lake Memsabok, south of the beautiful temple city of Palenque. The third village is on the southeast shore of Lake Na'ha (a Mayan name meaning "Mother of Water"). Lake Na'ha is situated about midway between the town of Ocosingo to the west, and Bonampak to the east. The Lacandons of Na'ha are the least culturally unadulterated of the three groups.

The villages are connected by long and difficult trails through the jungles. These pathways overlie the same routes trod by the Mayas as they faithfully journeyed from one ceremonial worship center to the other. Today, few of the visitors to the Lacandon Indians will challenge the hardships of the trail. They choose the airplane, which also presents an element of peril. Flying safely into and out of the crude and tiny clearings that have been hacked out of the jungle requires the skill and daring of the best of bush pilots.

Convinced that the overland experience would enhance an overall understanding of the Lacandon people, the author and his family elected to reach their destination of Lake Na'ha by trail from Ocosingo. The return journey was accomplished by airplane.

Seventy-two-year-old Chan K'in and teen-aged wife Number Three

Little Ky'um, "God of Song," — intelligent, talented and completely endearing

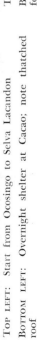

Top left: Start from Ocosingo to Selva Lacandon

Bottom left: Overnight shelter at Cacao; note thatched roof

Top right: Traveling through Ocosingo Valley

Bottom right: Estelle prepares evening meal; note slats for hut door

Top left: Chan K'in and his three wives

Bottom left: Gown worn by author woven by Chan K'in's wives

Top right: Chan K'in and part of his family

Bottom right: Estelle's birthday bouquet of jungle flowers given to her by son Jon

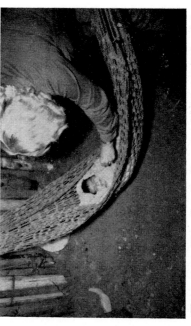

Top right: "Fuzzy" and wife, younger sister of Chan Nuk, Mateo's daughter

Bottom right: Baby rests in Lacandon hammock

Top left: Mateo (Chan K'in), his two wives and some of his children

Bottom left: "Puck" and wife; debris-strewn hut is typical

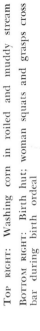

TOP RIGHT: Washing corn in roiled and muddy stream

BOTTOM RIGHT: Birth hut; woman squats and grasps cross bar during birth ordeal

TOP LEFT: K'in Bor and young wife

BOTTOM LEFT: Author with mother and baby, which he delivered

TOP LEFT: Bath time—an infrequent event
BOTTOM LEFT: Privy built by author; inquisitive lad has inspected pit interior

TOP RIGHT: Lacandon fife, drum, and rattle
BOTTOM RIGHT: Lacandon chicken coops save fowls from predators

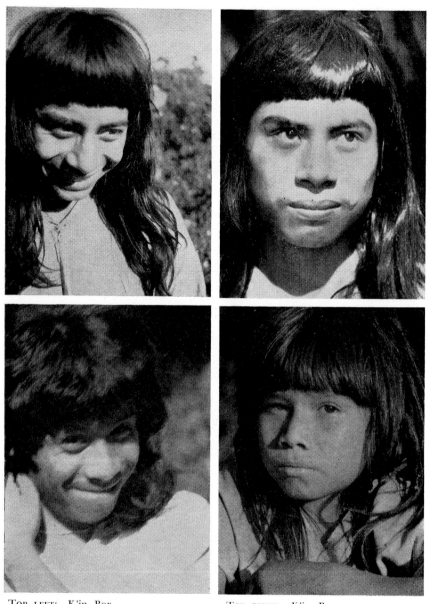

Top left: K'in Bor
Bottom left: Chan K'in, Jr.

Top right: K'in Bor
Bottom right: Chan Bor

TOP LEFT: A son of Mateo

BOTTOM LEFT: Baby enjoys snack after bath from rusty tin can

TOP RIGHT: Another son of Mateo

BOTTOM RIGHT: Lacandons in mahogany dugout on Lake Naʼhạ

TOP LEFT: Jon cruises Lake Na'ha in dugout canoe

BOTTOM LEFT: Harmonica music at nightly gathering in our hut

TOP RIGHT: Jon teaching Ky'um to sketch

BOTTOM RIGHT: Ky'um and burden of firewood; note tumpline on head

Top right: Newly cleared *milpa* (cornfield)

Bottom right: Fired clay pots being removed from wood ashes

Top left: Preparing molding clay for sacred animal figures

Bottom left: Chan K'in's wives tote corn; tobacco plants in foreground

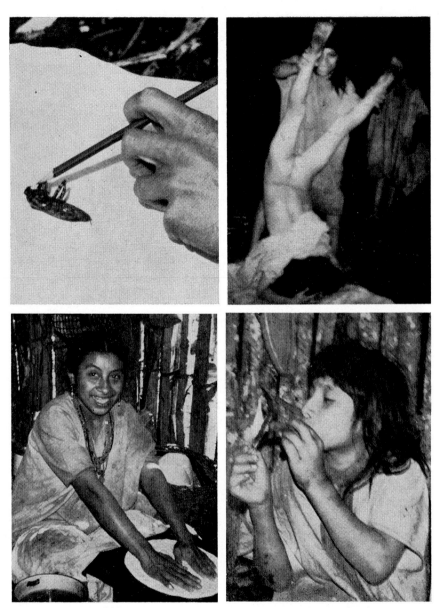

TOP LEFT: *Mokochi'ha,* poisonous flying beetle, tried to bite Jon

BOTTOM LEFT: Lacandon woman making tortillas

TOP RIGHT: Falling gown does not prevent attempt at headstand

BOTTOM RIGHT: Ky'um lights native cigar with flaming wood

Top LEFT: Girl's face disfigured by bullet wound

BOTTOM LEFT: Mateo, disfigured by fire at birth

Top RIGHT: Chan Nuk, seventy-one years old (Chan K'in's No. 1 wife)

BOTTOM RIGHT: Corn storage hut at a *milpa* (cornfield)

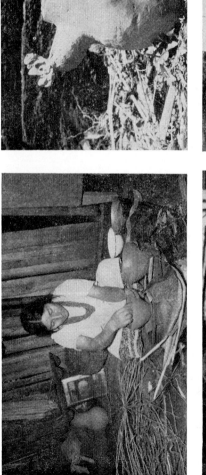

TOP RIGHT: Sacred pot will be made into a drum

BOTTOM RIGHT: Ancient customs prevail in crude loom and method of weaving

TOP LEFT: Lacandon woman shaping clay bowls

BOTTOM LEFT: Bark from special tree is pounded into barkcloth

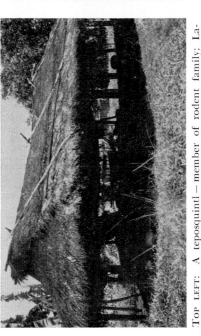

Top left: A teposquintl – member of rodent family; Lacandons' important food source

Bottom left: Sacred god house of Lacandons at Na'ha Village

Top right: Aerial view of Palenque, great ceremonial center of ancient Mayas

Bottom right: Feeding the gods during a ceremony in the god house

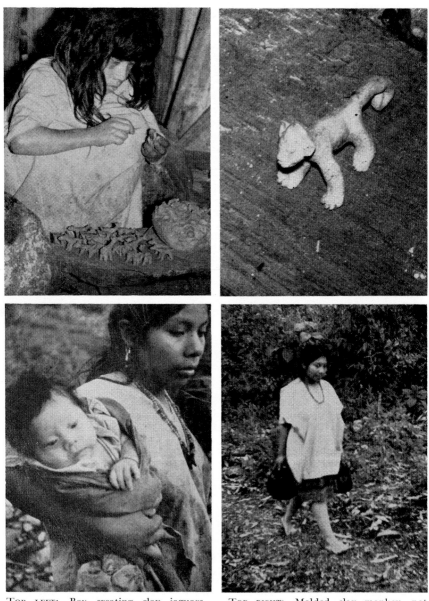

TOP LEFT: Boy creating clay jaguars, monkeys, teposquintl, etc.

TOP RIGHT: Molded clay monkey, not yet fired

BOTTOM LEFT: Oriental features of Mayas highlight baby's face

BOTTOM RIGHT: Girl carrying water in native gourds

Top LEFT: The deadly *nahuyaca* snake

BOTTOM LEFT: Pounding juices from ba-chol bark for sacred beverage

Top RIGHT: Basket weaving

BOTTOM RIGHT: Chan K'in constructing Lacandon drum

Top right: Cooking *Sa*, which will be consumed at sacred ceremony

Bottom right: Na'ha village from the air

Top left: A sacred bachol drinking fiesta in full swing

Bottom left: Chanting before two sacred god pots; smoke is from incense

Och (Aatch), four years old, smokes his customary evening cigar

Chan Nuk and the baby author helped deliver in emergency

A great deal of informa-
tion is available on the
subject of the once great
Maya civilization that
flourished in northern Central America, and mysteriously vanished nearly five hundred years

before the ships of Hernando Cortez and his expedition dropped anchor in the bay of Veracruz. Many of the scientific studies of the remarkably advanced Maya culture contain brief references to the Lacandons, one of the several tribal groups that structured the vast empire of the Maya.

Time, and the influences of modern civilization have drastically diluted and diffused the original characteristics of the Maya peoples. The Lacandons are the principal exceptions. They have consistently rejected major influences that would have materially altered their bloodline or their cultural heritage. Currently less than 150 in number, the extremely primitive Lacandons stubbornly cling to their ancestral gods and mores, and calmly await their approaching extinction.

Soon after completing an on-the-spot research of the cave dwelling Tarahumara Indians of northern Mexico, my family and I turned our eager attention to the Lacandons of Chiapas. It was mutually agreed that a study of their daily tribal life and customs would be a challenging and worthwhile endeavor. As had been the case in our Tarahumara adventure, if we were successful, we would be the first family team from the outside world to live in a Lacandon village.

In our explorations of the forbidding and barren Tarahumara country, it had been necessary that we travel several hundred miles on foot, backpacking all of our supplies and equipment.

2

Our trek through the mountains and jungles of Chiapas, to the Lacandon village at Lake Na'ha, would be accomplished on horseback. Pack mules would transport enough food, medicine, and other necessary supplies and equipment to sustain us independently for a minimum period of three months. Our return journey to the civilized world would be via the airplane.

I did not want to commit my wife, Estelle, and our son, Jon, to the very real dangers of a tropical jungle without first conducting a personal reconnaissance of the area directly involved. In June, 1971, Estelle and I went to Tuxtla Gutierrez, the state capital of Chiapas.

Arriving at the palace, or capitol building in Tuxtla Gutierrez, we met with Capt. Eduardo de Ganges, the military aide to the governor. The captain arranged an audience for us with Dr. M. Velasco Suarez, newly elected and installed as the state governor. An extremely busy, but very gracious man, Governor Suarez greeted us warmly, speaking to us in excellent English.

I explained the purpose of our proposed stay with the Lacandons at Na'ha village, and that the information gained therefrom would be incorporated in a book. "I have not yet visited Na'ha village," the governor said. "One hears many tales about the Lacandons. Most of the stories are filled with inaccuracies, and even fan-

3

tasies, I am sure. A true account of the Lacandons' life-style would be worthwhile. I offer whatever support that I can give you."

At one point during our conversation I inadvertently addressed the governor as "Doctor" Suarez. When I apologized, he laughed heartily, "I am happy that you called me 'Doctor'. I shall be the governor for only six years, but I will be a physician for the rest of my life!"

I wondered why a highly successful physician would turn his talents to the uncertain field of politics. Dr. Suarez's concern and compassion for the more than two million indigent people of Chiapas had prompted him to seek the tribulations of the governor's office. He is determined to institute lasting health and welfare programs at both state and federal levels for the primarily Indian population of his state. It will be a monumental and exasperating task.

The governor provided us with information on the diseases prevalent in the jungles, and among the Lacandons. He prepared a list of particular drugs and medicines that we should take with us, and included a detailed dosage schedule for each. He also gave us a letter of introduction, which requested all to whom it might be presented to respond to our needs with courtesy and dispatch.

4

San Cristobal de las Casas is located about fifty-three miles east of Tuxtla Gutierrez, and is the principal gateway to the Selva Lacandon. Over seven thousand feet above sea level, the city is nestled in a lovely, green valley of the Sierra Chiapas. Founded in 1525, San Cristobal de las Casas is a thriving city of 25,000 hospitable people, and is fast becoming a tourist mecca.

Governor Suarez had recommended that while in San Cristobal, we should talk with Professor Jose Weber, a noted teacher and historian. The professor was delighted with our plans to live with the Lacandons. He contributed a great deal to the ever-growing knowledge of what faced us during our forthcoming adventure.

In our avid quest for still more information, we turned to other citizens of San Cristobal. Displaying a natural fear of the unknown, most of the people with whom we talked held a common dread of the "wild" Lacandon Indians. They predicted that we were heading into a disaster. Several people recommended that we talk with Gertrude Blom, nee Duby, a longtime resident of San Cristobal, and well-known expert on the Lacandon.

Gertrude, or Trudy, as she is popularly known, is the widow of the late Dr. Frans Blom, a noted archaeologist who pioneered the exploration of the Selva Lacandon, and became the foremost expert on the Lacandon culture. Over a span of more than thirty years he collected a wealth of Lacandon artifacts which he placed on permanent display in his San Cristobal home. He also developed an outstanding library containing information on the Maya culture of the past. The library, too, is in his home, and is available to those with a legitimate interest.

Trudy participated fully in her husband's interests and activities. An authority on Maya culture in her own right, she is also noted for her outstanding photographs of the Lacandons and their jungle environment. Although there have been challenges to her sovereignty, especially from a young Canadian woman, the seventy-year-old Trudy remains the queen of the Lacandon.

Trudy speaks the Maya language fluently. She frequently enplanes to the jungle to spend days, or weeks, encamped near a Lacandon village. Acutely aware of the needs of the Lacandons, she has made many recommendations for their relief to federal and state officials. Not enough of them have been acted upon. However, Trudy was instrumental in the government's granting the Lacandons full title and rights to their lands.

Trudy personally supplies the Lacandons

with machetes, axes, picks, shovels, and other basic tools she thinks they will use. She has a concern for their medical welfare. On more than one occasion she has received word from the jungle that a Lacandon was seriously ill or injured, and made arrangements for airplane evacuation of the stricken individual to a hospital.

Paying guests are welcome to stay in her rambling, hacienda-styled home. Her chief source of income is derived from a "jungle escort service," which is rather expensive to use. Archaeologists, anthropologists, physicians, scientists, and others who are interested in studying the Lacandons or their environment, are escorted by Trudy to her jungle camps from whence visits are made to the Lacandon villages. Through her service, airplane flights are arranged for affluent tourists who desire a short-term snapshot adventure in the Selva Lacandon, and a return to San Cristobal in time for dinner.

We would not have need for Trudy's services, but we wanted to meet her. Our visit with her was of short, but revealing duration. We had no opportunity to ask questions — only to answer hers. Blunt, and painfully outspoken, she attempted to discourage our visit to the Lacandons. "The Chamula Indians live in the mountains just out of San Cristobal," she said. "Why don't you write a book about them?" During our stay with the Lacandons, we would learn more about this truly remarkable woman.

Our final activity in San Cristobal was to arrange for a morning flight to Lake Na'ha. Seated in a beautifully maintained, glistening Cessna "180," owned and piloted by Pepe Martinez, we were to be treated to an exciting demonstration of superb bush flying by one of Mexico's top pilots. It is no wonder that the Lacandon call him *Pepe,* the Mayan name for a butterfly.

Flying eastward over the densely forested slopes and foothills of the Sierra Chiapas, we saw vast sections of barren, useless land, horribly and permanently gutted by erosion. Pepe explained that these blighted areas were once Indian cornfields, or *milpas,* a term derived from the Aztecs.

In much the same manner as that employed by their ancestors of a thousand years ago, the various Indian tribes of Chiapas wrest the milpas from the jungle. Cutting and slashing a clearing with machetes, they leave the fallen trees, brush, and vegetation to dry. Later, the dried debris is burned, and corn is planted in the exposed soil.

After producing corn for two or three successive years, the thin layer of humus and topsoil becomes exhausted. The Indians then seek a new site to cut and slash, burn, and plant. The

8

abandoned milpa, without a protective cover, falls victim to the torrential seasonal rains. It is forever lost to the destructive forces of unchecked erosion.

Looking out of the windows of the airplane at the far-reaching landscape of beautiful green forests, interfused with starkly naked and gullied squares of land, I learned a vivid lesson. Maintaining a balanced ecology is not a problem uniquely reserved for the highly industrialized, overpopulated nations of the world. I recalled a remark made by Governor Suarez. "Unless we can teach the Indians proper erosion preventive measures," he said, "a great portion of beautiful Chiapas will become a wasteland within fifty years!"

As our flight continued eastward, we left the mountains and approached the Lacandon jungles. The jungle cover became more dense with each passing mile. About seventy-five air miles from San Cristobal, we cleared a high saddle ridge by a scant few feet and the plane swooped down over Lake Na'ha. Completely surrounded by low mountains, the small lake gleamed in the midmorning sunlight like a sparkling emerald. A few blobs of fleecy white clouds hovering overhead were perfectly reflected in the placid and clear waters below. A colorful panorama of lake, mountains, and clouds was beautifully mirrored on the polished undersurface of the airplane wings.

Pepe circled the plane over the lake twice, rapidly losing speed and altitude as he prepared to land on the small strip that began at the edge of the lake's north shore. The clearing did not appear long enough or sufficiently wide to permit a safe landing. As we skimmed low over the water, the aircraft responded to Pepe's delicate urgings as though it was a part of him.

The wheels touched down just beyond the shoreline and we jolted over the rough and ungraded terrain toward a mountain bluff that loomed ever closer. At the last moment the craft slewed sickeningly and did an abrupt about-face. We taxied slowly back toward the lake and stopped at midfield.

Four short and slender Indian men who were standing at the edge of the clearing walked toward the plane as we disembarked. I noted their almond-shaped brown eyes, the black hair hanging loosely almost to their waists, the knee-length, dirty white gowns that looked like ponchos, and the bare feet. We were looking at our first Lacandons.

Pepe introduced us to the eldest of the men, whom he called Jorge. Jorge accepted our handshakes, with a huge grin that revealed spaced gaps from missing front teeth. I was surprised that he spoke Spanish, but Pepe stated that nearly all Lacandon males could do so, but that the women could not.

On the top of a high hill west of the field, I saw several huts. East of the strip, and but a few yards from where we were standing, there were three crude dwellings, each covered with sagging, palm covered roofs. I walked to the doorway of one of the nearby huts and peered inside. A woman sat crosslegged on the ground beside a wood fire, preparing tortillas. She did not look up at me, but continued with her work. Two small, raggedly dressed children, their faces encrusted with dirt, timidly peeped at me from behind the woman. I entered the hut and offered the woman and the children several pieces of hard candy. When I left the hut to rejoin Estelle and Pepe, the two youngsters followed me. A taste of the sweet candy had melted their shyness.

Pepe explained that the main group of Lacandons resided in a village located on the southeast shore of the lake. It would be a long and difficult walk through a muddy jungle area, but if we so desired, Pepe said he would lead us to the settlement. We declined, as a visit would require several hours, and we were paying Pepe an hourly rate for his services. We took pictures of the Lacandon men standing by the airplane, gave them a few pesos, and boarded the plane.

11

Pepe taxied to the north end of the field, wheeled the ship around, and gunned it toward the lake. The Lacandon men were standing abreast at the edge of the field. As we bounced swiftly past them, Jorge raised an arm in a half-completed gesture of farewell. We circled the lake several times, spiraling upward to gain altitude. As we soared over the saddle ridge to the west of the lake I looked back. On the south-eastern shore I caught a brief glimpse of huts clustered in a small clearing. This would be the only view of the village until we returned to Lake Na'ha at year's end.

On our early morning flight to Lake Na'ha, a complete view of the far-reaching landscape had been obscured by many patches of fog. The hot, midmorning sun had burned away the shrouding mists, and on our return journey we could observe the full and wondrous beauty of the wild land below. Far to the south, on the Guatemala border, a mountain thrust its gleaming, snow-crowned peak far above the multi-green canopy of the sprawling jungle. Far ahead of the plane's nose, the Sierra Chiapas etched sharp and jagged silhouettes against the western horizon.

Our landing at San Cristobal signalled the end of the first important phase of our planning schedule. We returned immediately to our home base in San Antonio, Texas. Estelle and I spent

12

the summer months engaged in a television appearance and lecture tour of the western United States. It was not until November that we could devote our full attention to the procurement of food stocks and all of the many items and supplies that would be necessary to our expedition. At this time, Jon obtained a leave of absence from his school in San Miguel de Allende, Mexico, and joined us in San Antonio.

By mid-December we were ready to depart for the land of the Lacandon. All of the necessary permits and official papers were in our possession. When we completed the loading of our supplies and equipment in our motor home, it looked like an overloaded safari truck. We were caught up in a final whirlwind of parties and farewell dinners. As might be expected, a large number of people considered our ambitious project a dangerous, foolhardy venture that we might live to regret. There were others, however, who wanted to go with us. Surprisingly, more women than men volunteered.

We celebrated Christmas on the outskirts of Mexico City, with a poor family living in a one-room adobe hut. New Year's Eve found us in beautiful Veracruz, on the coast of the Gulf of Mexico. We toasted the newborn year with keen anticipation. If God willed, and the Lacandons cooperated with us, we would succeed in the fulfillment of a long-standing, fervent ambition.

The day after we arrived in Tuxtla Gutierrez, we were summoned to the government palace. There we met with the governor, and members of the television and news media. We were interviewed and televised with Governor Suarez as he presented Estelle with an autographed copy of a large book that contained color plates on the known birds of Chiapas.

Our scheduled departure for San Cristobal was postponed when I suddenly developed a dental illness that required emergency treatment, plus four days of precious and fleeting time. It was a painful setback, yet a fortunate one, indeed. I trembled when I thought of the possible consequences for my family and me had the abscess felled me at Lake Na'ha, nearly one hundred and fifty miles away.

In San Cristobal, we called upon Señor Humberto Zebadua, a local businessman and rancher, whom we had met the previous June. Señor Zebadua recommended and arranged for a Hermanjildo Gomez, an experienced and reliable guide, to meet me and my family on Thursday, January 20, in Ocosingo, a small hamlet about fifty miles northeast of San Cristobal. Hermanjildo would bring with him three saddle horses and a like number of pack mules. In the course of the

14

foregoing arrangements, an additional five days were sliced from our timetable. We resigned ourselves to the inevitable. Time is seldom rushed in Mexico.

We departed for Ocosingo early on Thursday morning. We had been assured that the unsurfaced route was in good driving condition. It proved to be the exact opposite. The heavy seasonal rains, now terminating, had left the mountain roadstead a shambles of washouts, potholes, deep ruts, and tire gashing rocks. On a soupy, mud-slimed curve our vehicle slid sideways, out of control. The six-ton motor home crashed into a huge boulder lying in the road. Luckily, the slow-speed impact did nothing more than crumple the vehicle entrance step.

It was late afternoon when we drove into the small outpost village of Ocosingo. The rough, unpaved main street led us to the central plaza, where we parked in front of the town's only church. Large plants, even small trees, had established precarious root holds and were growing out of cornices and crevices in the church's moss-covered sixteenth century façade.

Hermanjildo Gomez, our guide, was to have met us at the church. He was not there. While we awaited our guide's arrival, Father Bates, a member of the Dominican staff, led us on a tour of the historic house of worship. Later, at the invitation of Fr. Paul Duffner, the church director, we enjoyed a delicious dinner with him and members of his staff. Estelle, Jon, and I ate heartily. It would be a long time before we would again have the pleasure of eating steak, potatoes, and homemade bread.

It was after sunset when we left the dining room and returned to the motor home. We found it surrounded by a milling throng of children and adults. It was evident that the citizens of Ocosingo had never before seen a motor home. By nightfall, it seemed that every person in town had come to inspect and admire the strange American "bus," and the equally strange three *Norte Americanos.* We were honored with a surprise visit from the town mayor and his wife. They expressed a concern for us during our jungle sojourn, and wished us good luck.

Our guide made his belated appearance late Friday afternoon. Short, slender, and bowlegged, Hermanjildo was more than seventy years of age, exactly how old, he did not know. The wiry old man's gnarled and weatherbeaten face reflected his predominently Indian ancestry. In a mongrel Spanish, he apologized for his tardiness, tersely explaining that he had encountered serious difficulties in rounding up the horses and mules, which he had obtained from several outlying ranches.

16

Hermanjildo entered the motor home and examined the nine large, jute cargo bags we had purchased in San Cristobal. He approved of them, and gave us explicit instructions on packing the bags with our supplies and equipment. We were to have them ready for loading on the mules by sunrise the next morning. Hermanjildo left us, and we did not complete packing the cargo bags until well after midnight.

At the first glinting rays of the rising sun, Hermanjildo, astride his own mount, led a string of three saddled and bridled horses and three harnessed pack mules to the motor home. Bringing up the rear of the column on foot was a diminutive boy. He was Hermanjildo's grandson and named Alfredo. The thirteen-year-old lad would serve as the old man's assistant on the trail ride to Lake Na'ha. I wondered how such a fledgling of a boy could be of significant help on the forthcoming long and difficult journey. When I mentioned that there was no horse for Alfredo to ride, the old man shrugged and said that a horse would be available at Rancho San Antonio, our first day's destination. Until we arrived there, Alfredo would walk.

Jon and I helped load the pack mules. Three of the heavy cargo bags were balanced and lashed to form a pyramid on each mule's packsaddle. The mules were smaller than the American va-

17

riety, yet they were larger than the burro. The animals protested the heavy loads and noisily grunted their objections when the wide leather straps girting their bellies were repeatedly tightened and finally secured.

When the last mule was loaded, we took some photographs of the animals, and were ready to depart. I drove the motor home to the rear of the church building, where it would remain parked in the security of a walled and locked enclosure. The vehicle keys were left with Fr. Duffner for safekeeping.

During the bustling activities preceding our departure the people had been gathering on a nearby corner of the village square. As Hermanjildo led us single file out of the plaza, the gallery of curious townfolk were treated to an impromptu one-man rodeo. My mount, a nervous and headstrong bay gelding, wanted to lead the animal train. He exploded into a series of bone-jarring bucks that almost unseated me before he peacefully took his position at the end of the file. There were mingled shouts of "Bravo!" and "Adios, Amigos!" from the spectators as we rode past.

Flanked on each side by fog-shrouded mountain ranges, we followed a rain-gullied jeep and oxcart road that wound eastward through the wide Ocosingo Valley. The skies were cloudless

18

and the sun was hot. Our greatest discomfort would come, not from the heat of the sun, but from our blistering saddles. We did not look forward to this first day's ride of more than twenty-five miles.

A few miles out of Ocosingo we stopped to shorten the stirrups on Estelle's saddle, which were causing her some painful problems. Hermanjildo tried to correct the length of the stirrups, but failed. He said that they could not be shortened without a major saddle rigging alteration. Since this could not be done until we reached Rancho San Antonio, the poor girl would have to suffer the blistering consequences. All of the saddles were constructed in the same manner, otherwise Jon, or I could have traded with Estelle.

Jon and I were fortunate that the saddle stirrups were of the proper length. My chief problem was due to my not being conditioned to ride a horse; however I was determined to withstand the battering inflicted upon me by the unyielding leather seat. That Jon was not an experienced horseman was a fact soon discovered by his mount. From then on, there existed a constant battle of wills between them. The horse usually emerged as the winner.

The pack mules were not connected by leading ropes but were free to follow the horse ridden by Hermanjildo. Whenever a mule strayed to nip at a succulent clump of grass, it was Alfredo's duty to run after the errant beast and chase it back to the trail. Throughout the long, hot day the little fellow ran more than he walked, yet he never faltered or complained.

During the morning hours we met several Indian men who were walking to Ocosingo. They stepped off the trail as we approached, smiling and nodding to us as we rode past. Hermanjildo maintained a fast and steady pace. He rarely looked back at us. If we lagged far behind, he would not stop and wait for us. We soon learned to keep up with him, for urging our horses into a fast trot in order to catch up did not ease the blisters and sore muscles we had accumulated.

We had a brief rest at noon. The animals munched shelled corn out of nose bags. We hurriedly gulped cheese sandwiches, washed down with water from our canteens. The moment we finished eating and sprawled on the ground to rest our aching bodies, dour Hermanjildo grunted that it was time to mount up. All afternoon we continued to crisscross the Ocosingo Valley, which was fast narrowing between the flanking mountain ranges. We arrived at Rancho San Antonio shortly after sunset.

Our welcome was most hospitable, as Señor Zebadua, the ranch owner, had promised us back in San Cristobal. The ranch foreman provided us with a meal of scrambled eggs, beans, and tortillas. After dinner we were shown to a small windowless room containing three folding cots with springs made of rope, upon which we spread our sleeping bags. Before I went to bed I helped Hermanjildo make the necessary alterations to the stirrups of Estelle's saddle.

I also examined and treated Estelle's sores and bruises. The poor girl had suffered a great deal because of the too-long stirrups. In an attempt to ease the pain of broken blisters on her seat, she had tucked her soft-leather boots into the loops from which the stirrups were suspended. This only added to her misery. The edges of the stiff leather loops chafed and cut into her ankles, producing raw bruises. Determined trooper that she always is, she had not complained throughout the day-long ordeal.

We were up before sunrise, and enjoyed another ranch meal of scrambled eggs, beans, and tortillas, cooked on a primitive stove of mortared stone. We gave the woman cook a packet of cheese from our supplies as a present. This was a rare delicacy, so far from a market. When we finished eating in the windowless, earthen-floored, adobe kitchen, Estelle pressed a few pesos into the elderly cook's hand. The woman was still protesting the gratuity when we mounted our horses and rode out of the ranch house yard. At the trail's beginning, we looked back at the sprawling ranch house and outbuildings. The kindly foreman, a knot of ranch hands, and the cook were waving good-bye.

We had gone but a short distance when I yelled for Hermanjildo to stop. One of the mule's pack ropes had loosened and the cargo sacks were slipping dangerously to one side, threatening to slide completely under the animal's belly. I could visualize the frightened beast kicking frantically to rid itself of the bulky obstacles beneath him, and destroying one third of our precious supplies.

Well-versed in such emergencies, the old guide quickly reloaded the cargo sacks on the packsaddle. He pulled on the pack strap that encircled the mule's belly. The brute resisted by inhaling deeply and then holding his breath. This tactic did not fool Hermanjildo. He held the belly strap taut and patiently waited. When the mule could hold his breath no longer and abruptly exhaled, the old man swiftly took up the slack in the belly band and secured the cargo.

Our second day's goal was El Real, a large ranch located about twenty-three miles from Rancho San Antonio. The terrain became increasingly more difficult to travel and the streams deeper and more turbulent. The frequent river fordings were perilous at best. The sure-footed mules had no trouble in wading the shallow water crossings, but the horses frequently stumbled on the polished rocks of the stream beds. In deep waters, the horses, with riders aboard, swam easily across. Struggling under the weight of the cumbersome cargoes, the mules fought to gain the opposite shore.

We met a party of three Tzeltal Indians who were walking westward, probably to Ocosingo. Ahead of them they herded an enormous white pig. The hog was thickly coated with trail mud and black slime, and appeared to be in a state of near exhaustion. I wondered how far the pig had been driven, and if it could survive the many miles to Ocosingo.

Threading our way along a densely jungled ridge, we came upon the remnants of what had once been a Maya temple. Many such sacred temples have been found in the lands that once comprised the Maya empire. There are hundreds more lying hidden in the dense overgrowth of the jungles, still to be discovered. Nearly all of the temples that have been found have been reduced to heaps of useless rubble, thoroughly sifted by the greedy hands of plundering treasure hunters. Museums of the world pay handsomely for genuine Mayan artifacts in good condition, and rarely is the seller asked where and how he obtained possession of the treasure.

23

It is safe to assume that seventy-five percent of the priceless Mayan relics excavated and found in Mexico have been illegaly removed from the country. Despite tough Mexican laws against smuggling historical artifacts out of the country, the piracy continues. The smuggling of Maya treasure has not been confined solely to adventurers and treasure seekers. Many men, from many countries, including Mexico, have been, and are still involved. The methods of illegal removal are varied and ingenious. In 1971, an American archaeologist was arrested by Mexican authorities. He had carefully and skillfully machine-sawed a large, Mayan-sculptured and -designed, stone figure into a number of cross sections. The sections were to have been individually smuggled by airplane into the United States, and reassembled at the final destination.

We did not linger at the ruins. Hermanjildo wanted to go on. He guided us off the ridge to a valley floor, where a crystal clear stream danced and purled over shining white, yellow, red, and black stones. We stopped at the water's edge for our noon break. The animals ate corn, and we managed to eat some unsavory Mexican canned sardines and stale crackers. We fervently hoped for an extended rest period, but the ever impatient Hermanjildo had us back on the trail within thirty minutes.

A few miles from El Real we saw the mangled

remains of a small airplane lying amid splintered and broken trees. A short distance from the twisted wreckage a crudely fashioned wooden cross marked the grave of the unfortunate bush pilot. The accident had but recently occurred, for the fast-growing jungle had not yet blanketed the somber and barren grave mound.

The open pasture lands surrounding the ranch buildings of El Real were a welcome change from the obstacles of the jungle trail. The rigors of the day's ride had left their marks on all of us, including the little Alfredo, and rawhide tough Hermanjildo. There had been one after another of steep mountain climbs, slippery and dangerous descents, and slogging through the sticky, stinking quagmires of the choking jungles. Had we known that the worst was yet to come, we might have ended our adventure at El Real.

For many years El Real has been famed for its hospitality to the exhausted traveler. The guests have spanned the gamut from desperate cutthroats with a price on their heads, to zealous, soul-hunting missionaries. We received a warm and friendly welcome at the ranch and were treated to a supper of eggs, beans, tortillas, and fresh papaya. We were then assigned sleeping quarters in a wing of the ranch house. Hermanjildo and Alfredo cared for the animals and bedded down in a shed adjacent to the ranch's small airstrip.

25

Before going to bed we disengaged the ticks that had attached themselves to our bodies during the day. I treated Estelle's broken blisters and swollen, badly lacerated ankles. Wracked with pain, and utterly exhausted, she slept fitfully, tossing and turning during the night. I was seriously concerned about the wisdom of her traveling any further, at least for a few days. In the morning, however, she insisted that she felt much better. She vetoed my suggested delay and was anxious to go on.

Forty-five minutes out of El Real, we arrived at Yashoquintela, a jungle survival training camp and language school established by the Wycliff Bible Institute. I was happy to see the radio transmitting tower at Yashoquintela. Should an emergency befall us while we were at Lake Na'ha, the radio would be our nearest source from which to call for help from the outside.

Our unheralded arrival at the camp disrupted a class being conducted on the Tzeltal Indian language. During the ensuing recess we were surrounded by students who were happy to see and talk with someone freshly arrived from the United States. An extended visit at Yashoquintela would have been of great interest, but we remained but a few minutes. Time was of the essence. At the camp store we purchased some oranges and tangerines, and a replacement cargo bag for one that had become badly torn on the trail. We enjoyed a drink of cool, clear water and rode away.

The route we followed after leaving Yasho-quintela became so terrible that by noontime we knew that reaching Lake Na'ha that day, as planned, would not be possible. With a measure of luck, we would arrive instead at an Indian village called Cacao before nightfall. We had little time to reflect upon our disappointment. Just staying in the saddle required our full attention.

The way became a nightmare that drained the strength of man and beast alike. While fording a swift river, a mule slipped and fell into the swirling, angry current. I was sure that the struggling, frightened animal would be swept downstream and lost. Miraculously, it managed to regain its footing and scrambled to safety. The packs were soaked, but otherwise in good condition.

The final mountain obstacle we encountered was indeed formidable. To enable the horses to ascend and descend the precipitous and rocky trail, we frequently had to dismount and walk behind our mounts, sometimes holding to their tails for support and assistance. The mules with their heavy loads, fell often. One fell backward, down the mountain, and did a complete somersault, suffering only minor cuts and scratches. I shall never

27

forget those horses and mules — such magnificent, stouthearted, and willing animals.

After crossing the mountain range, we entered the jungle lowlands of the Selva Lacandon. The open trail soon became a dark, narrow tunnel that had been macheted through solid foliage. The ceiling was so densely matted with growth that the sun's rays could not shine through. A massive and continuous web of vines bristling with cruel thorns clutched and jabbed us painfully as we pushed through. The tunnel sides were solid walls of trees, thorny vines, and brush. Our knees and legs were battered and bruised from being slammed into tree trunks as the horses bucked and plunged through thick, belly-deep mud.

At one point along the trail, Alfredo was bringing up the rear of the column. He came running up behind me on foot. His horse had become stuck fast in the mud, and would I help free the animal? I turned my horse, and followed the boy to where his frightened horse was trembling in deep mire. Its legs were entangled in a spidery mass of vines that were buried deep in the mud. I probed in the black muck with my hands to find and sever the entrapping vines with my heavy hunting knife. Once freed, the desperate horse lunged his way clear.

It required ten hours to travel the fifteen miles

from El Real ranch to Cacao. Cacao's entire population was housed in four thatched huts. When we trooped into the village it appeared deserted. As we were dismounting, an Indian man came out of a dwelling. He watched us for a moment and reentered the hut. Hermanjildo walked to the hut's door and talked to someone inside. The old man returned and led the horses and mules to a small shelter at the edge of the village clearing. The shelter had no walls, and a thinly covered roof of palmetto leaves. It afforded a minimum of protection, and no privacy.

Our gear and supplies were stacked at one end of the dirt floor space. The remainder of the area served as a sleeping ground for all of us. This was to be the first night that we would not sleep in a complete building as we had at the ranches. We spread our sleeping bags on the ground but neglected to erect our mosquito nets. This was a foolish oversight on my part, but I was too tired to think, or care. We were under attack all night from mosquitos, ants, and spiders. The stench from the sweat-soaked saddle blankets Hermanjildo and Alfredo were lying on only compounded our abject misery.

We departed from Cacao early on the morning of January 24. The fog was extremely heavy. Moisture fell from the overhanging branches of tall trees and pattered on us like rainfall. We had

29

enjoyed clear and sunny weather thus far, but Hermanjildo assured us that through the month of February, we would have much fog, and sporadic, fierce wind and rainstorms.

The five-hour ride to Lake Na'ha was exhausting. All during the punishing morning we constantly pestered weary Hermanjildo with "How much longer before we reach Na'ha?"

The stern old man's answer was always the same. "Una hora!" The fog soon burned away under the hot sun, except in the low valleys where it clung like great blobs of white cotton. We wound our way through a dark forest of sapadillo, mahogany, and huge, knobby-kneed cypress trees, and forded a swift stream. On the opposite bank we entered a high screen of reed grass. When we emerged from the reeds, we were on the edge of the airstrip at Lake Na'ha. We were too tired to yell our elation. All we wanted was to get out of the saddle and stand on our own feet.

Across the field from us were the three Lacandon huts Estelle and I had visited the previous year. On the western side of the field, almost hidden in thick foliage, was a small open-walled shelter consisting of upright poles supporting a palm leaf roof. Flowing beside the shelter, a stream originating at Lake Na'ha, rippled over a bed of polished stones and white gravel. A foot bridge of three parallel poles spanned the water, ending at the foot of a trail that led up a steep hill. At the top of the hill were two native huts and a small bungalow.

We led the animals to the shelter, but did not remove the loads from the tired mules. I first wanted to obtain permission to camp under the shelter's protective roof. Three young Lacandon men were standing atop the hill watching us. Jon and I walked up to meet them. Perhaps they could tell us from whom we could get permission to use the shelter.

One of the Lacandons was dressed in an ordinary modern-styled shirt and a pair of almost new blue jeans. He was also wearing a pair of slightly worn manufactured leather sandals. We would later learn that the young nonconformist had partially succumbed to the missionary influence, and had adopted civilization's mode of attire, in addition to some of the outside world's less attractive modes, such as stealing and dishonesty.

We were trying to converse with the young men when a white man stepped from the bungalow. He was a missionary. He and his wife, who did not come out of the house to meet us, had lived on the hill for several years. At the moment, they were in the process of packing. They would be leaving Lake Na'ha the next morning.

31

The missionary informed us that we must gain permission to use the shelter as a campsite from a Lacandon man known as Jorge, who lived in one of the three huts adjoining the eastern edge of the airstrip. This would be the same Jorge whom Estelle and I had met on our brief visit to Lake Na'ha the previous June. As for the prospect of our living in the village, we were told that the Lacandons residing there were not noted for their hospitality. Unless they invited us to move to the village, it would behoove us to leave Lake Na'ha.

Jon and I returned to the shelter. We did not have to go and find Jorge. He was already on hand, talking to Hermanjildo. Jorge remembered me and shook my hand. He granted us permission to camp under the shelter. Hermanjildo unloaded the pack mules and Jon and I hung the cargo sacks from roof poles, thereby lessening the chance of rats molesting the food.

We pitched our tent under the thatched roof of the shelter. It was an incongruous arrangement, but practical, for it would give us additional protection from the elements. Everything that could not hang from the roof poles was stored inside the tent. Our sleeping space was cramped, but critical items of equipment were out of the weather, and more secure against pilfering.

Our contract with Hermanjildo expired when

we arrived at Lake Na'ha. After unloading the mules and unsaddling the horses, he turned them loose to graze on the thick grass that bordered the airstrip. I questioned the wisdom of permitting the animals to roam freely, unhobbled and unattended. Hermanjildo assured me that the beasts were too tired and hungry to stray from the immediate vicinity of the shelter.

There were still several hours of daylight remaining when we finished organizing our camp. I was anxious to go to the village. Hermanjildo said that he knew some of the men at the settlement, including the leader. When the old guide offered to escort us to the village, I eagerly accepted.

Estelle and Alfredo remained at the camp. Jon and I followed Hermanjildo to the lake end of the airstrip. He led us to a trail that began on the northeastern side of the lake. We walked the trail but a few yards and came to a group of small, well-built shelters clustered in a cleared area of the jungle. The largest shelter had a stove made of adobe. There was a plank table with a bench on each side. The shelter was obviously a combined kitchen and dining area. There were three small shelters with hard-packed earthen floors that were designed for use as sleeping quarters, with hammock poles erected in each.

Hermanjildo said that the camp belonged to

33

Gertrude Duby. I compared our rickety shelter in the open to Trudy's snug harbor in the protective cover of the jungle. Jon remarked that her camp would be much more comfortable. I knew what he was thinking, and I thought of the same course of action. We both agreed, however, that if Trudy had wanted us to use her camp, however temporary our stay might be, she would have invited us to do so. We would not change campsites.

We left Trudy's enviable camp and followed Hermanjildo over a darkly shadowed and muddy trail. After about one and a quarter miles the gloomy pathway topped a high and sharp ridge. About two thousand yards below the ridge we saw the clearing and the simple huts of Na'ha village.

A committee of viciously barking dogs greeted our entrance into the Lacandon settlement. Except for two women standing at the far end of the village, there was no one else to be seen. The largest of the huts was located in the center of the clearing. Hermanjildo told us to wait outside, and he strode through the open doorway. We could not see anyone inside the dark interior, but we heard Hermanjildo conversing in his peculiar Spanish. Several minutes passed before our guide rejoined us. Behind him came a wizened Lacandon man not more than five feet tall. He was obviously quite old, yet he walked with a

34

surprisingly fluid and easy grace. His dark and heavily wrinkled face was framed in a loose cascade of black hair that reached well below his stooped shoulders. A tuft of coarse hair bearded a pointed chin. The prominence of his broad flat nose was somewhat diminished by large, almond-shaped brown eyes that peered from deeply cratered sockets. The old man wore the typical Lacandon male sleeveless gown, handwoven of cotton. The incredibly dirt-encrusted, once-white garment stopped short of the man's bony knees. His short legs were dark and scrawny and he stood on bare, splayed feet.

Hermanjildo introduced him as Chan K'in, the recognized leader of the Lacandons of Na'ha village. We let Hermanjildo tell him the purpose of our coming to Na'ha. Chan K'in spoke directly to me but once. Were we missionaries? I shook my head in the negative and said that we were not. When Hermanjildo told Chan K'in that my family and I wanted to live in the village to learn the ways of his people, the old leader said that after he conferred with the men of the village, a decision would be made. He then turned from us and walked into his hut. The all-too-brief powwow was ended.

During our face-to-face meeting Chan K'in's eyes had frequently studied me. There had been no hostility in his steady, penetrating gaze, nor any curiosity. I felt strangely drawn to the serene and mysteriously magnetic primitive. Had I chanced to meet Chan K'in anywhere, even out of his native jungle environment, I know that I would have sought this man's friendship.

We arrived back in camp at dark. I felt that the meeting with Chan K'in would prove successful and we would be invited to move to the village. Estelle and Jon could not completely share my optimism.

At sunrise a plane landed, picked up the waiting missionary couple, and departed. The entire operation did not take more than fifteen minutes. Our guide had also expected to leave very early that morning, but a serious problem had developed during the night. The unhobbled horses and mules had vanished. The old man and his grandson made numerous but futile searches in the surrounding jungle. Estelle, Jon, and I did not join in the hunt for the missing animals. Our saddle sores and bruised legs and knees kept us quietly in camp.

The horses were found at ten o'clock. It was high noon when the mules were discovered on a trail several miles east of the airstrip. Hermanjildo and Alfredo ate a hurried lunch and were ready to leave. I thanked the old man and his grandson for their excellent services and paid Hermanjildo the full amount we had agreed upon before leaving Ocosingo. He pocketed the money and then claimed that since he had been unable to leave early that morning as he had planned, I owed him money for an extra day.

Outraged, I asked Hermanjildo to explain more fully. In a sad, almost tearful voice, the old pirate said that he had rented the horses and mules by the day at a certain number of pesos per head. Because the unfettered and unguarded animals had wandered away, it had cost him an additional half day to find them. It would be a grave injustice if he had to pay for the unfortunate delay in his schedule out of his own pocket. Further, he reasoned, he would not be at Na'ha, and in this dreadful position, if it were not for us! Therefore, all things considered, I should bear the additional expense. I am not mentally nor emotionally equipped to combat such logic. I paid. Estelle and Jon laughed at my frustration, telling me that I had fallen victim to the trap neatly set and sprung by the uneducated but cunning old trader.

We watched the two riders and the column of animals file into the wall of jungle and disappear. We were now alone in a vast and hostile wilderness, under the constant scrutiny of a tribe of primitives. What if the Lacandons did not accept us? I thought of many things that could happen to us, and dismissed them from my mind. I was confident that our mission would be accomplished.

C H A P T E R 2

While awaiting word from Chan K'in, we idled away the time in camp, recuperating from the punishing trail ride. We bathed, and washed our soiled clothes in the nearby stream. Taking a bath was always a fearful and nervous experience, for the heavily reeded and brushy banks of the shallow, but swiftly flowing stream were infested with a variety of poisonous snakes. At first, bathing was also an acute embarrassment. Standing in knee-deep water while soaping and rinsing our naked bodies, we presented a full view to any curious Indians who might be peering at us through the thick foliage along the banks. As the days went by, we ceased to be self-conscious and began to enjoy the delights of bathing in nature's soothing bathtub.

Several young boys who lived by the airstrip were frequent visitors to our camp. They would silently file into the shelter and sit cross-legged on the ground with their gowns tucked beneath their knees. Our attempts at conversation with them were fruitless, since they spoke only Maya. They answered us with smiles, and would join us in laughter when our ludicrous sign language got out of hand. They loudly smacked their appreciation of the hard candy we gave them. When the candy was consumed, the youngsters would not ask for more, but would run across the airstrip to their homes.

One afternoon I was busy excavating a deep trench around the borders of the shelter in preparation for the rain that was overdue. I was using a combination pick and shovel tool that I had brought with the supplies. While I was working, Jorge came by for a visit. I welcomed the chance for a rest and a smoke. I smoke a pipe, but I had brought in several cartons of cigarettes to ration piecemeal to the Lacandons. I offered Jorge a cigarette. He accepted it with a snaggle-toothed smile of appreciation. When I returned to the task of digging, Jorge took the shovel from my hands and finished the trench.

I noticed that Jorge was wearing a handsome, gold wristwatch. Where, or how he got it, I do not know. While he worked on the drainage trench, he stopped every few moments to raise his arm in an exaggerated gesture of importance to stare and frown mightily at the timepiece. I saw that the watch face was being worn upside down. This made no difference to the squinting Jorge. He could not tell time.

Thursday had been a beautiful, warm, and cloudless day. Late in the afternoon we heard an eerie, high-pitched sound rising from behind the mountains to the north. The awesome noise came rapidly closer. A ferocious wind suddenly stormed over the ridges, screaming through the trees like a horde of demented banshees. With the gale winds were angry black clouds and torrential rains. We were being subjected to one of the frightening storms Hermanjildo had warned us would come.

41

Less than two minutes after the storm struck, the land was engulfed in almost total darkness. A cracking, splintering crash near us signalled the assaulting wind's victory over a towering mahogany tree. The avalanche of rain continued without letup. The penetrating cold, surprising in a tropical jungle, sent us early to the snug warmth and comfort of our air-cushioned sleeping bags.

The skies dawned clear on the following morning. The sun peeped shyly over the eastern mountain rampart, its blush casting a subdued rosy glow over the placid waters of the lake. Jon and I were nursing a sick fire with small slivers of wet wood. Three young Lacandon men, breathing heavily, suddenly appeared at the shelter. Chan K'in had dispatched them via dugout canoe to fetch us, and our belongings, to Na'ha village.

We gulped a skimpy breakfast and quickly struck camp. The young men helped carry the heavy cargo bags the considerable distance to the dugout landing point. There was room for all of our gear, the three Lacandons, and us in the mahogany dugout. Estelle cannot swim. She looked at the unsteady craft lying very low in the water and cast another look at the wide expanse of Lake Na'ha. She asked me to walk with her on the trail to the village. Jon remained with the dugout.

Estelle and I were a long time on the muddy trail. Our progress was held to a snail's pace because of the rains of the night before. When we entered the village, we saw our supplies piled on the main pathway through the village, in front of Chan K'in's hut. Jon, covered with black mud, and obviously agitated, was waiting for us. I asked him what had happened. "We crossed the lake in less than twenty minutes," he said. "When we arrived at the landing area, the three Lacandons carried some of the cargo from the dugout to the village. When we got here, the men of the village were holding a meeting. The three who were with me joined them. They are all in there." He gestured toward Chan K'in's dwelling. "They are really upset about something. They are all talking at once, in Maya, and I think the conversation is about us."

I asked him how he had become coated with mud. After the boat crew had deserted him, he had unloaded the dugout. While struggling toward the village with the heavy and cumbersome loads, he had fallen several times in the lakeshore's odious black muck and mire.

A young man dressed in a clean white gown appeared in the doorway of Chan K'in's hut. Speaking in Spanish, he gruffly asked us to come in. We filed into the hut. A circle of stony-faced men were seated on the hard-packed dirt floor.

Their gowns were tucked under crossed knees. One of the men was old Chan K'in. The grim looking Lacandon who had asked us to enter the hut was the leader's eldest son. His name was also Chan K'in. (As a means of easier identification, future reference to this young man will include the title of "Junior.") He was a slender and wiry young man, and about five feet, four inches in height.

Chan K'in, Jr. was the core of the serious problem that confronted us. He had been absent from the village on the day that Jon and I had met his father. When he returned, his father had already made the decision to invite us to come to the village. His son persuaded several of the men who had approved of his father's action to change their minds. The critical conference had been called by the young hothead and would develop into a final showdown.

Estelle, Jon, and I stood apart while Chan K'in, Jr. talked to the assembled men in rapid-fire Mayan. Turning to us, the hostile and suspicious fellow asked why we wanted to stay in the village. It was difficult to understand his Spanish. In turn, he was baffled by our stumbling answers. Only after a laborious and painful effort at a partial understanding of the letter of introduction given to us by Governor Suarez, did the scowling Chan K'in, Jr. soften his aggressive, angry at-

44

titude. The office of governor carries a great impact in Mexico, even in the heartland of a jungle wilderness.

Chan K'in, Jr. conferred at some length with his father, speaking loudly and with passion. As he had been throughout the entire meeting of the group, old Chan K'in remained serenly composed, calmly puffing on a fat, native tobacco cigar. When his son yielded the floor, the old man spoke to the assembly. The men eyed each other as he spoke and nodded their heads in collective approval at the end of his deliberate, but softly delivered talk. What had struck me as the sitting of a kangaroo court was suddenly adjourned. The verdict was in our favor. We would stay in the village. As a small token of appreciation I doled a cigarette to each man. The Lacandons filed from the hut, blowing clouds of smoke and grinning their pleasure.

Chan K'in, Jr., who was now quite amiable, walked with us to our stack of supplies. He pointed to a shelter standing in the center of the village and apart from the family dwellings. He told us that we would stay there until a hut could be built for us. Work on the hut would begin on the morrow. When completed, it would be the first dwelling at the northern limits of the village.

The young man finished talking to us and left us to our own devices. As I watched the haughty

45

primitive stalk away, I realized that we would need to cultivate this temperamental firebrand very carefully. The success of our mission would depend greatly upon our gaining, and keeping, his confidence and trust.

We carried the supplies and equipment to the appointed shelter, which was much like the one we had used across the lake, but perhaps more delapidated. Our first order of business was to carefully inspect every item we had brought to Na'ha, particularly the food stocks, for damage or deterioration. In a wet, highly humid environment, rifles, knives, and other articles of metal require daily and meticulous care against rust and corrosion. Clothing, canvas, and leather goods will quickly mildew and rot if neglected. Precious photographic equipment and film must receive special upkeep and storage.

Except for an insignificant amount of food items that had been damaged on the trail, our possessions had survived the ordeal in good condition. Our inventory disclosed that one flashlight was missing. It had been in our possession when we arrived at Lake Na'ha. Some time later, one of the village youths told us that it had been stolen while we were camped on the lake's north side by the shifty-eyed young Lacandon in sandals and blue jeans who lived on "missionary hill."

46

We replaced our food stocks in the cargo bags and suspended them well above the ground in what we hoped would be a dry and rat-free area under the palm leaf roof. Everything else was stored inside the tent, which was pitched beneath the shelter. We completed the organization of the camp by digging a deep, rain drainage trench around the perimeter of the shelter.

With our temporary dwelling arrangements completed, we had the first opportunity to look over our surroundings. Na'ha village is built on rather steeply sloping ground, and about 500 yards from the lakeshore. The trail from the airstrip winds through the center of the village clearing and continues southward over the mountains. Worn pathways led from the main trail to eight dwellings, which were quite far apart. Some of the huts had walls of rough planks split from mahogany logs. The other huts had walls of small poles placed in the perpendicular. All of the dwellings were roofed with palmetto leaves. None boasted a window. The doors consisted of removable upright slats of split mahogany. There were no chimneys. The smoke from the perpetually burning wood fires escaped through gaps in the walls, and also filtered upward through the layered leaves of the palm roofs.

Hard by the clearing's eastern boundary stood a large, open-sided structure. It was covered with a low, ridged roof of palmetto leaves that had turned moss-gray from the elements. This was the sacred hut, or god house. Until we became better acquainted with the Lacandons, or until we were invited to visit the place of worship, we would not go near it. To do otherwise would be to invite certain and serious trouble.

Off the village pathways grew tall grass and brush. All of it was entangled in choking vines. In the central village area there were several orange and lemon trees yellowing with ripening fruit. Mango and papaya trees were in the start of seasonal bloom. A small grove of rubber trees which would shade our hut when it was completed, leaned their towering heights down the slope toward the lake.

Water for the village gushed crystal clear and pure from a limestone spring located uphill on the north boundary of the clearing. No one lived above the water source, and the Lacandons did not go to the site. They obtained water about thirty yards below the spring, where the rivulet tumbled into a pool about three feet in depth, and four feet in diameter. The Lacandons had split lengthwise an eight-foot length of bamboo pole. They had scraped out the soft inner core of each half to form two troughs. These were anchored parallel to each other in midstream, with the lower trough ends protruding a few inches past the upper edge of the pool. The women could easily and quickly fill gourds and other containers with small openings at the perpetually flowing twin water spouts.

During the first several days we were in the village the inhabitants ignored our presence, and avoided us as they went about their daily pursuits. The cockroaches were not so reticent. Hordes of the noisome pests came scurrying through the vine-choked grass to invade our camp. Strangely, they never found the food cache hanging from the shelter roof poles. The tent was their main objective. Although we kept it tightly closed, the roaches managed to gain entrance, going to the extent of cutting three large circular holes in the rear wall. We squashed them by the hundreds every day. Oddly, after we moved to our hut, the roaches were no longer a problem.

Flying insects and bugs were an ever-present irritation. We were bitten and harrassed by gnats, flies, ants, and mosquitos by day. At night, fleas and mosquitos tormented us. Ticks buried their toxic heads in our flesh at all times. Tiny, biting gnats were our greatest problem. Clouds of the black demons attacked us constantly throughout the day, ceasing their assaults only after sundown. Insect repellent only served to whet their appetites. Too small and swift to swat, they bit quickly and flew away, leaving behind spots of oozing

49

blood and a severely painful itch. Many times we would brush a hand across the forehead or the back of the neck and draw it back covered with blood.

Jon and I have a natural immunity against the toxic effects of insect bites. The intense itching quickly recedes and there is little, or no swelling. Estelle is not so fortunate. Within a few hours she became so welted, swollen, and feverish from the insect bites that I considered sending a Lacandon runner to Yashoquintela with a message to radio Pepe Martinez to fly in and evacuate her to a hospital. Estelle dissuaded me from my intent, for she was determined to stay at Na'ha. Fortunately, she improved under the medication I had available, and in a short time she developed a tolerable measure of immunity against the toxic reaction of the insect bites.

On Saturday evening, January 29, the sun disappeared behind a blood-red horizon. Soon thereafter, a velvety dusk swiftly dissolved into the enveloping gloom of the jungle night. The creatures of the light fell silent as the denizens of the dark began their stealthy reign of terror. In a little while a full moon, immense and majestic, swept slowly above the darkly silhouetted eastern mountains. The soft, searching beams first kissed the shimmering waters of the lake before gliding

50

up the slope to paint the weathered, gray palmetto-fronded roofs of the village huts a silvery lustre.

The wild, pristine panorama was a scene of unutterable beauty. Deep within my being strange passions clamored for expression. I wanted to shout with joy at nature's absolute and eternal magnificence. At the same time, tears stung my eyes because of my mortal nothingness. As I stood under the vault of the star-studded heavens I thought of the millions of human beings who live in metropolitan jungles of brick, glass, and asphalt, and who never see the stirring beauty of a moonlit night because of the grimy, veiling haze of their manufactured pollution.

The Lacandon families had sought the security of their huts when dusk had ended. When we at last went to sleep, the village was quiet but for the sad whining of a tethered dog. Shortly after midnight we were awakened by a bedlam of sounds. Indians were yelling and running wildly in every direction. From all about the village came the wailing and crying of women and children. From the nearby god house a mixed chorus of eerily chanting male voices brought an icy tingle to the nape of my neck.

I fumbled nervously with the zipper of the tent flaps. I asked Estelle to remain in the tent as Jon and I stepped outside to look warily about.

51

Jon nudged me and pointed to the moon. It had passed its zenith and was beginning its western descent. The sky was cloudless. A black curtain was slowly drawing across the face of the moon. The right quarter of the lunar face was almost lost in toal darkness. The remaining area was veiled in an angry red color that was slowly fading to a murky amber.

An unusual number of shooting stars streaked through space in the area surrounding the moon. We were witnessing the early phases of a total eclipse of the full moon, a phenomenon my family and I had never observed. The eclipse was the reason for the Lacandons' terror-stricken behavior. The end of the world was at hand, and unless the gods intervened, mankind was doomed. Nobody would live to see the sunrise. The pandemonium in the village lasted well beyond the nearly three hours of the eclipse time.

After the long night of terror the Indians went about their normal routines as though nothing had happened. The gods had once again thwarted the evil plans of the god of the underworld, and all was well. At sunrise a slender Lacandon man came to our shelter. His name was also Chan K'in. He would be known to us as Mateo. At fifty-four years, he was the second oldest man in the village. Like the other adult males, he could speak Spanish.

52

Mateo's first impact upon us was somewhat unnerving. Behind the tangles of long hair was a hideously disfigured face. His forehead was heavily scarred, and he had no eyebrows or lashes. One ear was missing. The lobe of the other was gone. There was no upper lip, and his yellowed teeth protruded from exposed and shrunken red gums. Where his nose had once been there were two ragged-edged, pink cavities. Mateo had suffered the terrible accident on the night of his birth. A clay pot, filled with fiery wood coals, had been placed beneath his mother's hammock to keep her and the newborn infant warm. While his mother was asleep, he had fallen from the hammock, face first into the pot of coals.

The Lacandons accept without stigma one who is deformed or ugly. Mateo was a happy man. He possessed two wives (a third had died), was the father of many children, and was an influence among his people second only to the recognized leader, old Chan K'in.

Mateo had come to the shelter to invite Jon and me to accompany him and two young men on a work party. We would cross the lake by dugout canoe, walk to a valley in the mountains, and bring back enough palmetto fronds to roof our hut. We welcomed the chance to help the Lacandons. The hut was now framed and the completion of the roof would hasten the day of occupancy.

Jon and I shouldered our machetes and a camera, and followed Mateo and the two young men down the swampy trail to the lake. At the water's edge were two long dugout canoes. They were tied by short lengths of vines to an upright pole that had been anchored in the deep mud. The young fellows boarded one of the crafts and untied the vine from the stake. One sat in the bow, and the other stood upright in the stern. They paddled out to deep water and waited for us. Jon and I sat in the bottom of the dugout. Mateo stood in the stern and wielded the crudely carved mahogany paddle with smooth and skillful ease. With our dugout leading the way, we glided toward the western shore.

Mateo had taken an immediate liking to me. He offered me a fat cigar, rolled of native-grown tobacco. The tobacco tasted sweet, but the smoke was strong and biting. I looked with some apprehension across the beautiful blue waters of Lake Na'ha to the vegetation-choked shoreline. I asked if there was possible danger from alligators. Mateo said that there were a few small ones in the lake, but that they seldom ventured from the marshy shore areas. He said that a small lake nearby was literally filled with alligators, many of them very large, and all of them very hungry.

When we reached the matted shoreline, Mateo stood in the bow and slashed a lane through the vegetation with expert sweeps of his sharp machete. We secured the dugout to a branch of a fallen tree and walked its trunk to step ashore. The young men tied their canoe to ours and joined us. With Mateo in the lead, the Indians cleared a narrow pathway up a steep slope. The going was slow and cutting a passageway was difficult. Jon and I volunteered to relieve the young men. Our machetes were clumsy and heavy in our inexperienced hands, and we made but little progress. Smiling broadly, the fellows resumed the trail cutting. Jon and I fell to the rear, where we had the going much easier.

When we were descending the opposite slope of the steep ridge we had been climbing, the column suddenly stopped. Looking ahead, I saw Mateo holding a hand to his head. A rivulet of blood was streaming down his forehead and face. While slashing at hanging vines that barricaded the way, his machete struck a large tree. The resounding blow had dislodged a dead limb dangling high in the tree. The jagged end of the falling branch struck Mateo squarely on the top of his head and left a deep and ugly laceration.

I soaked my handkerchief with water from my canteen and applied it directly to the wound. A few minutes of constant pressure stopped the bleeding. I washed the blood from Mateo's face, rinsed the handkerchief, and folded it into a narrow band. The makeshift bandage was placed on the cut, and the ends tied under Mateo's chin. The young men thought the sling looked very funny and laughed uproariously. Mateo could not see the comical arrangement, but he laughed with them.

Periodically I poured water on the bandage to prevent the cut from becoming dry and crusted. When we returned to the village I would clean it and treat it properly. Mateo appreciated my concern for his well-being. He gave me two more cigars.

After the accident we moved on to a small valley where we found a grove of denuded palmetto trees. Mateo had been there two days before and lopped off the fronds. He had stacked them neatly in three separate rows for today's baling and removal to the village. One of the men searched for and found a particular type of tree. He chopped it down and removed the pliant bark in long, narrow strips. The strips would be used to tie the palmetto leaves into bales. In the meantime, the other fellow cut four slender poles into four-foot lengths. He sharpened one end of each, and pushed them into the soft earth to form a rectangle about two feet by three feet in size.

Jon and I gathered small sheaves of palmetto fronds from the piles and handed them to Mateo, who placed them in layers between the upright poles of the rectangle. When the bale of leaves reached a height of about four feet, it was secured around both ends and the middle with strips of bark. The tied bale was set aside while work commenced on another. I lifted the finished bale and estimated its weight to be at least ninety pounds. After several bales had been compressed and tied, Mateo began to carry them up and over the high ridge, and down the other side to the waiting dugouts. I watched the seemingly easy manner in which Mateo placed the heavy bale on his back. He first kneeled on the ground with his back to the bale. He adjusted a loop of bark around the load and across his forehead, then rose to his feet. With both hands free, he swiftly disappeared in the direction of the dugouts, and soon returned for another bale of palmettos.

Jon and I wanted to do our share. He was the first to kneel with his back to a bale. He adjusted the bark tumpline around the load and across his forehead. When he tried to stand, he could not get his knees off the ground. Grins of amusement creased the handsome faces of the two young Lacandons, as I helped my son gain his feet and stand upright. The huge bale swayed precariously side to side. Straining and stumbling, Jon careened forward for several yards and collapsed in a grotesque sprawl. Our companions' grins changed to irrepressible howls of laughter.

The men eyed me expectantly. Would the

57

toted the bundle down the main village trail. We stopped frequently to rest or get a fresh grip.

The Lacandons had returned to the village from their work in the milpas, or cornfields. Men and boys were idling in the shade of the huts. As we stumbled past a cluster of keenly interested onlookers, we lost our balance and fell. The Indians' response was immediate. It was not a derisive or ridiculing laughter, but a spontaneous outburst of genuine humor induced by our ludicrous tumble. When we laughed with them, an important link was forged in the growing chain of understanding and friendship.

The next day we watched the palmetto fronds being converted to a roof for our hut. Three men worked on the rooftop, skillfully placing the leaves with the stems toward the peak, and in overlapping rows. The stem of each frond was tied to a cross pole with vines and strips of bark. Mateo, the tireless workhorse, kept the roofers supplied with leaves, carrying them from the ground to the men by way of a unique ladder.

The construction of the ladder emphasized the native ingenuity of primitive children of nature. It consisted of a pole, twelve feet long, with a diameter of six inches. Evenly spaced, deep notches had been chopped the full length of one side of the pole. The pole was leaned against the hut. His arms loaded with palmetto leaves, Mateo scampered nimbly up the notches as though they were wide, solid steps. Unencumbered with a load of leaves, I attempted to walk up the pole. The unanchored pole turned under my feet and spilled me to the ground. Jon suffered the same fate.

When the roof was completed the upright poles forming the walls were tied in place. Narrow widths of split mahogany were fitted loosely between parallel poles tied horizontally at the top and bottom of the entryway at the front and rear of the hut. The huts of the Lacandons have no interior walls or partitions. We had the workmen depart from custom and divide our fourteen-by twenty-feet dwelling into two rooms, with an opening between.

Chan K'in, Jr., whom we had seen very little, joined the work force. He built a pole bed for Jon against the north wall of the front room, which also served as the kitchen. Against the south wall of the rear room he constructed a double bed for Estelle and me. I helped him in a small way by holding the poles in position as he secured them with strips of bark. Since our first unpleasant meeting, the impetuous firebrand's attitude had mellowed considerably, and we were becoming quite good friends.

We moved into the hut on Wednesday, the second of February, five days after our arrival in

60

the village. That night a howling rainstorm struck. Jon's sleeping bag was soaked as the whistling wind blew the rain between the poles of the north wall. The roof leaked like a sieve. We had not dug a run-off trench around the base of the hut. The water flowed ankle deep across the dirt floor. It was a long, wet, and cold night.

It was still raining hard the next morning. We huffed and puffed enough heat from a weak, wet-wood fire to cook a meagre breakfast of pasty oatmeal. At midmorning, two of the front door slats were removed without warning, and Chan K'in, Jr. squeezed his body inside. He quickly surveyed the leaking and flooded hut and left without a word.

Shortly thereafter, the three young men who had constructed the roof filed into the hut. Their long, wet hair was plastered tightly to their heads and clung to the contours of their necks and shoulders. Water dripped from the hemlines of their soaked gowns. They greeted us with wide smiles and examined the leaking roof.

Chattering in Mayan, two of the men went outside and climbed to the rooftop. The third remained inside, and indicated the leaking spots by pushing a stick up through the palmetto leaves. As he moved back and forth checking the entire roof area, his bare feet churned the floor into a sea of mud. Much of the sticky mire was de-

61

posited on the bunks when he stood upon them to probe the palmettos. The men worked swiftly and rearranged the overlapping of all the leaves before the leaking stopped.

We were to experience no more trouble with the roof. Chan K'in, Jr. apologized for the slipshod manner in which the hut had been built. For the rest of our stay in his village, the structure would remain a thorn of embarrassment to the sensitive young primitive.

The cold rains drenched the land for four days and nights. Soon after the return of the drying sun, we completed our housekeeping arrangements. To make living and working conditions more comfortable, and also to keep all supplies and equipment off the ground, I constructed shelves, kitchen and bedside tables, and corner tables. I copied the Lacandons' methods of construction and used small poles fastened together with vine and bark strips. Large, flat-topped rocks were used as stools. As the cargo bags were emptied, they were converted to floor mats.

When our new home was in order, we were free to pursue our study of Lacandon life on a full-time basis. Each of us had definite work assignments. Estelle would log her daily experiences, concentrating her main efforts on the Lacandon woman's role in the family structure. Her gentleness and compassion would enable her to open feminine doors to information that a prying, curious male could never hope to unlock.

Jon, the artist, was charged with sketching, still photography, and tape recording of various tribal activities, ceremonies, etc. He would, in addition, maintain a daily journal, recording the customs and habits of the Lacandon youth. My tasks were of an overall responsibility. I would keep detailed notes of what I observed and learned. The capturing of important events and activities on movie film was my task.

Although we were invited guests, we were strangers in the village. The people ignored us and generally left us completely alone. If we were to gain their genuine friendship and trust, we would have to make the first moves. We began by visiting the homes. We tried being very correct when we paid a visit to a hut. If the door slats were in place, we knocked. If the entryway was open, we stood on the outside and announced our presence. Neither method was successful. We soon adopted the uninhibited way of the Lacandons, and that was to simply walk in without any sort of preliminaries whatsoever. We were usually greeted with a smile, but since most of the people spoke only the Maya tongue, conversation was held to a bare minimum. We were always given permission to photograph the interior of the huts and the activities of whomever might be inside.

63

The contents and arrangements of the dwellings were generally the same. The only items of furniture were crude sleeping pallets placed in corners, or along a wall. The pallets were made of poles and mahogany slats, and stood about two feet above the ground. None had mattresses or blankets. Some of the children's beds had pieces of tattered and dirty rags that were too small to cover a sleeping child.

The sleeping arrangements of a Lacandon family are worthy of note. The children sleep on pallets. If a man has but one wife, they sleep together on a pallet. Men with more than one wife sleep alone in a hammock made of handwoven, heavy cotton cords. The hammock is suspended between two poles placed upright in the center of the hut.

The interior squalor and filth of the huts was appalling. The earth floors were always littered with trash and debris, consisting of corncobs, dried corn husks, partially burned pieces of firewood, ashes scattered from the ever-burning fireplace, broken bits of pottery, feathers, and droppings left by chickens which regularly coursed through the huts. There were never any food scraps or bones. Such discards were snatched up by the hungry dogs as soon as the items were thrown to the ground.

Fleas were everywhere, and on everybody.

64

One day, Estelle and I entered a hut and saw a mangy, yellow dog lying outstretched on a pile of corn husks. A scrawny, bare-necked chicken with its tail feathers missing was walking slowly back and forth on the sleeping dog's body, methodically pecking fleas from the disinterested beast's hide. Whenever we were close to a Lacandon man, woman, or child, we could see the fleas jump in a flying arc from the individual to us.

Every night, just before going to bed, we made an attempt to de-flea ourselves. Invariably we overlooked one or more of the little pests. Their presence, and bites, would not be felt again until after we were snugged into bed. We sprayed insect repellent and flea powder on our sleeping bags, and every day that the sun was shining they were hung outdoors on a rope. None of these measures were successful in controlling the flea population entirely. They were a necessary evil, and we resigned ourselves to that fact.

The Lacandons, of course, had no bathroom, or toilet facilities. The nearby screening jungles served the needs of all but the very young, who would relieve themselves wherever they happened to be when the urge compelled. When we had first arrived in the village, I had macheted a trail into the jungle and cleared a small site that served as our toilet area. Going to the "comfort clearing" from our hut entailed a hundred-yard walk,

65

sometimes a sprint, with an entrenching shovel in hand. Hordes of biting insects always awaited our arrival. The possibility of being suddenly confronted by a poisonous snake while in a temporarily helpless position was very real.

As soon as we were settled in our hut, I set about constructing an outdoor toilet. The privy would stand downslope and a reasonable distance from our dwelling. The door would face Lake Na'ha. The thin layer of humus and topsoil of the Na'ha region lies on a formation of soft limestone. Digging the pit for the toilet was most difficult and required almost a week of exhausting and hand-blistering effort.

The Lacandon adults paid little heed to what I was doing, although they must have wondered why I was digging such a deep hole. The children could not withstand their natural curiosity. Single, and in pairs they frequently came and sat on the ground nearby, watching as I burrowed ever deeper. Two of my most regular visitors were Chan K'in, four years of age, and his three-year-old half-sister Chan Nuk. They were members of old Chan K'in's large family. Because of the many "Chan K'ins" in the tribe, we called little Chan K'in "Och" (pronounced "Aatch") the Mayan term for baby.

When the pit reached a depth of five feet, I turned my attention to the building of the toilet

66

box and seat board. I built the box of closely fitted poles tied together with strips of bark. A wide rough plank split from a mahogany log was selected as the seat board. I had planned but a single hole in the board. With thoroughly feminine and indisputable logic, Estelle convinced me that there should be two holes, just in case of a double emergency. Limited to the use of my hunting knife, it required two days to whittle and carve the twin holes in the thick mahogany plank. A pole frame and a slanting roof were erected over the toilet and covered profusely with palmetto leaves. The door had upper and lower sections that opened independently on their heavy vine hinges. Both of the door sections were also covered with palmetto fronds. The finished product was a rainproof, and practically peek-proof privy of which I was justly proud.

Estelle and Jon encouraged me to photograph my improvised masterpiece, the first toilet to be built in the jungle village of Na'ha. I walked to the privy with a camera and found one young Lacandon looking at the structure. I measured the light reading, set the distance and exposure, and raised the camera to my eye. I was pleased at what I saw. The late evening sun was streaming through the opened doorway, bathing the mahogany seat in golden splendor. My finger reached for the shutter release. Without warning, a

Lacandon boy's head popped up through the nearest toilet hole. The sudden emergence of the impishly grinning face startled me and I instinctively triggered the camera release. The result was one of the most fascinating and hilarious candid pictures I have ever taken. The inquisitive lad had entered the toilet pit to get a worm's eye view of my handiwork.

The palm covered toilet proved to be well worth the sweat, toil, and blisters I had endured. It served its purpose adequately. The lack of a mail-order catalogue to thumb through was more than compensated for by the gorgeous view of the lake as observed through the opened upper section of the double door.

I hoped to persuade the Lacandons to build several toilets as one important means of disease and parasite control. I attempted to explain to Chan K'in, and his eldest son, how serious diseases were transmitted by flies, roaches, and other carriers, including polluted water. Several days later two men, under the supervision of Chan K'in, Jr. began digging a pit downhill from the huts. They excavated the hole to a depth of about three feet, and stopped digging. When we left Na'ha eight weeks later, nothing more had been done. I was disappointed, but not surprised. Primitive peoples are very childlike. Like children, they may become excited and even enthusiastic over something new, or different, but their attention span is short-lived and the object of original excitement is quickly forgotten.

The Lacandon generally do not wash their clothing. In fact, they seldom remove their clothes for any reason, even sleeping. The people do not bathe. Mothers will bathe the babies perhaps once a week, concentrating the cleansing effort on scrubbing the wee bottoms with a rag that has been dipped in a clay bowl, or a bent and rusted tin can containing water.

On the hottest days the older boys and the young men climbed into a dugout and paddled away from the marshy shore to where the water was deep and clear, where they dived in for a momentarily cooling swim. Jon and I accepted several invitations to accompany the lads on a canoe ride and a swim. Our young hosts ignored our repeated demonstrations of a heavy lathering of soap, followed by a rinsing dive into the waters of the lake. Their interests were primarily cooling ones, rather than cleansing.

Our family bathing and laundering routine was unique. The rivulet that flowed from the limestone springs near our hut was too small and shallow to permit either bathing or the washing of clothes. We used the large stream flowing from the north end of Lake Na'ha, where we had encamped on our initial arrival. We walked the three-mile round trip every other day, with Jon going on one day, and Estelle and I on the next. The bath and wash days contained an element of peril, for inevitably we saw venomous snakes along the trail, and sometimes at the stream. The dreaded fer-de-lance was the most dangerous threat.

The *nahuyaca*, as the fer-de-lance is called by the Lacandons, grows to a length of seven feet, or longer. It has a yellow belly, and a distinctive yellow-bordered diamond-shaped pattern on its dark green back. The head is large, flat, and square-nosed, and the tail is very thick with a blunt end. The nahuyaca is very difficult to see because its blend of colors and design complements the surrounding foliage of the jungle. It is usually found lying closely parallel to the trail, or behind a fallen tree trunk that spans the pathway. The reptile strikes swiftly and repeatedly, without warning. Death comes to the victim within perhaps ten or fifteen minutes, as the venom affects the nervous system. Many Lacandons die from the bite of this silent killer. The barefooted and bare-legged Indians' best defense is constant alertness.

CHAPTER 3

According to our careful census, a total of sixty-six men, women, and children resided in the vicinity of Lake Na'ha. Of this number, thirty-nine individuals lived in Na'ha village, twenty-four resided on the lake's north side by the airstrip, and a family of three lived in the mountains south of the lake.

The Lacandons of the village held the people who lived on the lake's north shore in rather low esteem. There was very little direct communications with them. Chan K'in's utter dislike and mistrust of missionaries contributed greatly to the lack of community rapport between the two groups. Those individuals on the north side who had been noticeably influenced by the exhortations of past missionary efforts, such as the theologically and socially confused young man who wore the clothing and sandals of the outside world, were held in contempt by the unbending adherents of the Mayan beliefs and customs. As an example, the young man referred to in the foregoing sentence was not welcome in the village unless he was attired in traditional Lacandon dress.

Of the Lacandons who lived by the airstrip and on "missionary hill," only Jorge appeared to enjoy a measure of respect and acceptability by those of the village. We did not meet the man and his two wives who lived in isolation south of the village. None of them visited Na'ha, although one of the women was Chan K'in's sister. It was undoubtedly a case of exile for the recluse and his wives, but the true facts were never disclosed to us.

Among the Lacandons there were but six

male names, and three female names. Chan K'in was the predominent title bestowed on the males. The majority of the females were named Chan Nuk. Learning to differentiate many persons with the same name was a most confusing task. To make individual identification easier we resorted to the use of nicknames.

The proper names of the Lacandons are of Maya origin, and each has a distinctive interpretation as indicated below:

MALE	FEMALE
K'IN: *Sun*	NUK: *Big*
CHAN K'IN: *Little Sun*	CHAN NUK: *Little Big*
BOR: *God of Music*	KO: *Animal Spirit*
CHAN BOR: *Little God of Music*	
K'IN BOR: *Sun and God of Music*	
KY'UM: *God of Song*	

Gaining the Lacandons' confidence was at first a one-sided effort that required a great deal of patience on our part. It was primarily through the ready friendship of the children that we were

73

able to dissolve the invisible barrier that divided us from the adult population. The childrens' first shy peepings at us from the security of their huts soon progressed to lingering walks past our hut. It was not long before the lure of candy treats had the youngsters stopping briefly for a daily visit.

The first important breakthrough in our relations with the people came about because of Jon's dedication to Yoga exercises. In the dusk of evening, he spread an empty cargo sack on the ground in front of our hut, and used it as an exercise mat. One of the usual exercises was a headstand.

The unfamiliar sight of a man standing on his head for a long period of time with his legs and body unmoving was more than three boys, who had been watching discreetly from a distance, could bear. They converged on the scene and sat on the ground to watch. After a few moments of silent staring at the upside-down Jon, they began to chatter rapidly among themselves. One of the lads laughed openly. His companions immediately joined him. The three were soon holding their sides in unrestrained glee. Jon completed the headstand and the boys departed. A few moments later we heard a commotion nearby. The three boys were in an open area, trying unsuccessfully to stand on their heads. Whenever one of them fell backward, to fall on his bottom with a resounding thud, the others howled with laughter.

The boys returned to our hut on the following evening. They wanted Jon to teach them the headstand. Estelle and I sat on a rock, swatted mosquitos, and watched the fun. The boys discovered an immediate and sensitive problem. They could not attempt a headstand without their gowns falling and exposing their naked bodies. To circumvent this embarrassment, they held the hems of the gowns tightly between their legs with one hand. Trying to do a headstand with only one arm resulted in even more grotesque physical collapses and greater peals of laughter from the youngsters.

After two evenings of these uproarious antics, the boys gave up on trying to control the gowns. Having grown accustomed to us, they cast aside all modesty, placed both hands on the ground, lifted their legs skyward, and let the gowns fall about their heads. It became commonplace to witness a small, naked male body with its head on the ground and the legs uselessly churning the air for balance. Every day, the boys tried to stand on their heads, yet none of them ever succeeded.

Our friendship and personal attachment for the three boys grew rapidly. Chan K'in was eight years old, and the youngest. Next was Chan Bor, who was nine. The oldest of the trio was Ky'um, eleven years of age. All were sons of Chan K'in. Every evening, as the fireflies twinkled bright patterns in the deepening dusk, the three youngsters would be in front of our hut, trying headstands, wrestling, chasing each other, and behaving much as active nine to eleven-year-old boys generally do, with several unique exceptions. They never became angry or quarrelsome, and they never cried when they were obviously hurt.

When darkness mantled the village we moved indoors and sat in a close circle around the dancing flames of the fire. We gave each of the boys a nightly allowance of one piece of hard candy, which they devoured with noisy delight. Ky'um spoke Spanish, and we conversed with the trio through him. Our sign language technique became quite proficient also, for there were many topics of discussion for which we could not find the proper words. The boys were content to sit for long periods in silence. Now and then one of them would reach beneath his gown, capture a biting flea, and flip the tormentor into the burning coals. Some of the fleas escaped the fiery doom. We would find them later in our sleeping bags, where they would involve us in nightlong, frantic games of hide-and-seek.

The lads never explored our hut, nor touched any of our possessions. Sometimes they asked what a particular item was that they could see from their positions around the fire. On occasion, a good-natured wrestling match would erupt. A firm "No! No!" from one of us would end the roughhouse immediately.

The nightly fireside sessions normally lasted until eleven o'clock, when the boys would file out of the hut and return to their homes. The last one out would replace the slats in the doorway. We never tired of the youngsters' presence; in fact, we looked forward to the nightly assemblies. Uninhibited and unspoiled, the wonderful babes of the jungle were a joy to be with.

Little Ky'um became our favorite of the older boys. Sensitive, highly intelligent, and wise beyond his tender years, he captured our hearts. During the day, he spent every moment with us that he could. At night, when the other boys left our hut, Ky'um often remained for an additional hour or two.

Ky'um displayed a keen interest in the English language and learned many of the commonly used words. Watching Estelle, Jon, and me playing rummy, and listening intently as we audibly counted our scores, he learned to count a little. The young fellow was happiest when he was teaching us his native Maya language. Because of the many glottal sounds it is difficult to master, and our progress was slow. Ky'um was blessed with an enduring patience. When we would finally master a particularly difficult word or phrase, he would flash his dimpled smile and proudly exclaim, "Net'soy! Net'soy!" which in Maya means "Very good! Very good!"

One afternoon Ky'um was watching Jon sketch a village scene. He asked for a sheet of paper and a pencil. His crude drawing of some nearby trees and bushes revealed a surprising talent. Thereafter, Jon devoted much of his time, and precious art supplies, to teaching Ky'um the fundamentals of sketching. The two became inseparable. When Jon's sketching interests extended beyond the village confines, Ky'um led him to outlying areas in the jungle and mountains where he showed him food plants, berry bushes, flowers, trees sacred to the Maya religion, unusual insects, animals, and exotic birds.

Late at night, Jon often sat on a cargo sack on the floor and worked on his day's collection of sketches. Ky'um was always beside him, drawing on a piece of paper, or just watching his idol at work. Eventually, our supply of candles was exhausted. Jon and Ky'um then worked by the light of the fire, or from the sputtering yellow flames of a piece of burning mahogany pitch.

The frequently repeated scene of Ky'um struggling to produce a sketch that would bring praise from his beloved teacher was heartrending, indeed. Poor little Ky'um! He might have the talent of a Picasso, but his potential must remain unknown, to die with him one day in the jungle wilderness. Had he lived during the height of ancient Maya glory, Ky'um's art might well have graced a wall in a splendorous temple of the gods.

A poignant event took place one night that we shall never forget. We had completed an extended language lesson, taught by Ky'um. It was late, and the once red embers of the dying fire were turning an ashen gray. It was time for Ky'um to go home. He stood and placed a hand on Jon's shoulder. "I am your brother," he said softly. Turning to Estelle he said, "You are my mother!" He looked at me and solemnly said, "You are my father!"

The regular visits by the boys drew the attention of the young men of the village. First one, then another, invited themselves to our socials. At first, they were shy and uneasy in our presence, but after a few visits they became regular members of nightly gatherings. The young men were not interested in trying to do headstands. I introduced to them the sport of one-hand wrestling, wherein two contestants stand and try to win the match by throwing the opponent to the ground with only one hand. It was an immediate and lasting hit with the young men. I wrestled one after the other until my muscles ached from the strain.

79

I was never thrown to the ground by one of my young adversaries. They were as strong as bulls, but they did not understand the proper use of leverage and balance, the keys to winning a one-hand wrestling match. Once, in the struggle of a contest, I threw my opponent to the ground with enough force to stun him. He shook the cobwebs from his head, laughed, and came back for more. The fun-loving Lacandons did not care who won, or lost. The pure zest of the physical contests was all that really seemed to matter.

I was challenged to participate in the Lacandon style of wrestling. It is the ordinary method of wrestling, except that it is based on brute strength and stamina, rather than the application of subduing holds. In this rough and rugged form of entertainment, I took my lumps, and lost many matches.

The Lacandons' penchant for horseplay developed into some frightening experiences. The ringleader was a twenty-two-year-old, extremely handsome fellow named Chan K'in. He was the eldest son of Mateo. There was nothing the young man enjoyed more than frightening the three of us at every opportunity. We soon gave the inveterate prankster the name of Puck.

It all began very late one evening when we were sitting in front of our hut. Jon was lost in

80

deep thought. Estelle and I were a few feet away from him. A slight rustling came from the brushy area fronting our hut. In the semi-darkness I saw Puck stealthily creeping up behind the unsuspecting Jon. I signalled Estelle to not sound a warning, for I sensed what was about to happen.

When Puck approached within several feet of Jon, he emitted a blood-curdling yell, pounced on Jon and held him about the shoulders in a tight bear hug. Before the thoroughly frightened Jon could react, or even yell his terror, four boys came seemingly out of nowhere and grabbed his legs. Amid great shouts of triumphant glee, poor Jon was carried to the nearby stream of shallow water. Standing on the edge they lustily swung him back and forth as though to toss him bodily into the shallow creek, before placing him gently on his feet and releasing him. They trooped back to the hut with tears of laughter streaming down their bronzed cheeks.

I was not to be spared in these antics of fright. One night I was standing alone, admiring the stars. I was seized from behind by Puck. My desperate wriggles to escape were of no avail. He hoisted me to his shoulder like a sack of corn. My captor trotted on for a few yards then lowered me to my feet. He let me go, and ran laughing to his hut.

Late at night, when we were asleep, the rascal Puck would quietly sneak close to a wall of our hut. With a blood-chilling imitation of a prowling jaguar's roar, he would bring us bolt upright and trembling in our sleeping bags. Before any of us could compose ourselves, we would hear Puck's nearly hysterical laughter as he ran off. We could not get angry at his devilish pranks, nor could we retaliate.

Our good relationships with the children, the boys, and the young men soon paid real dividends. It was not long before the adult males were dropping in for a visit. And we found ourselves welcome to visit them in their huts. The Lacandon women call on a neighbor only during daylight hours, and then only if the husband of the hostess is absent. Estelle's female visitors clung to custom, calling on her when Jon and I were away from the village. Like the males, the women entered the hut without warning. Two of them walked in on her when she was taking a sponge bath. She maintained her composure and went on with her bathing, while the women inspected the interior arrangement of the hut. They were surprised and delighted with the tables, shelves, and the manner in which the kitchen was arranged.

The women of the village openly admired Estelle's honey-blonde hair. They were greatly intrigued by her red enameled fingernails. They wondered why she painted them, and were also curious as to why the red color would not wash off when she placed her hands in water.

Estelle's greatest problem with the women was the Maya language barrier. She partially surmounted this by a patient use of sign language. The Lacandons were drawn to her by her sincerity, warm and ready smile, and outgoing personality. She had brought a large collection of costume jewelry from the United States, to be given to the women as tokens of friendship. Each woman was free to select the bracelet, necklace, or earrings that pleased her most. Estelle soon had the gratitude and friendship of every young girl and woman in the village.

Two constant and always welcome daytime visitors were little Och and his half-sister Chan Nuk. The little girl dogged our every footstep, with her large brown eyes sparkling with excitement, and her tongue constantly a-chatter. It was of no matter to her that we could not understand her Maya prattle; the lovable little pixie was happy to carry on with her unceasing, one-sided conversation.

Och was the silent, serious type. He did not get under foot, but sat on the ground or on a rock and watched our activities. The only times that he came near us was when we handed him a piece of candy. The little fellow usually topped off his candy treat by smoking a cigar. I was never able to adjust myself to the beautiful, four-year-old child nonchalantly puffing on a huge cigar while studiously regarding me through veils of swirling tobacco smoke.

Our friendship with Mateo, the second senior citizen of Na'ha, had been firmly established on the day that I treated the scalp wound he suffered while gathering palmetto leaves for our hut roof. He came to our hut often, always bringing a gift of cigars for me, or three fresh eggs for my family's eating pleasure. I responded with gifts of cigarettes, the only items that I really had to offer, and which he was delighted to get.

Although we were overjoyed that so many of the Lacandons were coming to our hut for friendly gatherings, our main concern was gaining the complete acceptance of both old Chan K'in, and his son, Chan K'in, Jr. To that end, we made frequent calls on both of them in their respective dwellings, where we were always made to feel welcome. I was elated when the old man began to return our visits. And, the first time that Chan K'in, Jr. came by for a short social talk, my joy knew no bounds. I knew that we had finally and totally been accepted by him and his father on the night that he gave Jon and me permission to enter the sacred god house at any time to observe, photograph, and sound tape any religious event or sacred ceremony that might be taking place.

The Lacandons are a patriarchal society. The woman is little more than chattel, an item of valuable property first owned by her father, and later by her husband. Her chief roles in life are to provide sex and tortillas for her man, rear her babies, and toil endlessly from dawn until dark.

The Lacandon men marry women of their own tribe. Exceptions are extremely rare. The polygamous order made tracing the blood relationship of family individuals almost impossible. First cousins intermarry, as do uncles and nieces. In one case, the eldest of a young man's two wives proved to be his grandmother.

Males outnumber females at Na'ha. There is no courtship before marriage. A girl is sold by her father to the suitor who can afford to pay for her, or who will agree to a long-term installment contract of purchase. Inflation has invaded the remote jungles of Chiapas, also, for the current price tag on an unmarried female is about 3,000 pesos, or roughly 240 United States dollars.

A young Lacandon will not possess that much money. In order to purchase a wife, his only recourse is to somehow earn and save as many pesos as he can. This is accomplished primarily by making many bows, and hundreds of stone-tipped arrows. The completed bow and arrow sets are bundled and tied with vines, and carried on the young man's back over the many miles of jungle and mountain trails that lead to the market places of San Cristobal, or Tenosique. There he will sell the bows and arrows for a mere pittance to a dealer, who will retail them for a handsome profit to the ever increasing and avid tourist trade.

Over a period of many months, perhaps years, the young hopeful will make and sell enough bows and arrows to accumulate at least a down payment for a bride. The balance due on his verbal contract will be discharged by working for the girl's father. This will entail cutting, burning, and preparing jungle clearings for new milpas, cutting and carrying firewood, hunting game, and other tasks as specified by the girl's father.

The suitor may not claim his prize until the entire indebtedness is paid off. The time required to discharge his debt also serves as a probationary period. Should he fail to measure up to the criteria as established by the girl's father, the purchase agreement is voided. He cannot have the girl, and further, all cash and work he has invested becomes forfeit.

Because of the scarcity of females a man cannot always buy a girl who is old enough for marriage. His purchase may be a girl who may be only three, or four years of age. He must wait until the girl baby matures, usually at eleven or twelve years of age, before he can take her as his wife.

The token of marriage worn by the wife is a colorful feather ornament tied to the end of her single, long braid of hair. Soon after marriage, the husband goes into the jungle in search of a parrot, macaw, toucan, or other brilliantly plumed bird. He will kill it and fashion the token from the brightest feathers. The meat of the hapless donor of the feathers will be eaten.

A disgruntled husband cannot discard a wife unless her father agrees to take her back into his family fold. The husband must also pay a "riddance" price to the father. The return cost can range upward to 1500 pesos. One fellow who was unable to live in harmony with his wife negotiated a return agreement with his father-in-law. Not possessing the total funds for a cash settlement, the young husband made 1,000 arrow points to satisfy the balance due.

A wife cannot leave her husband without his consent. Should another man become seriously involved with a married woman, her husband will either kill him, or decide to give his errant wife to her paramour outright. In the rare event that he relinquishes his claim to her, his wife and her lover must leave the village, and remain banished forever.

87

A man who desires to have more than one mate must obtain permission from his first, or "number one" wife. Approval is normally granted. The more wives there are in the household, the less workload there is for wife number one. The first wife maintains complete authority over any additional wives she authorizes her husband to purchase.

Lacandon sex mores are loosely structured. Most boys are introduced to the mysteries of sex by the older females, often their mothers, or grandmothers. Girls learn the biological facts of life from youthful lovers. An unwed girl with a child suffers no tribal scorn nor penalty. Her life in the community goes on as usual. The Lacandons do not kiss or hug. Outward manifestations of affection are limited to touching lightly with the hands.

A husband with only one wife shares his bed with her. However, a man with several wives and a bevy of children, sacrifices all conjugal privacy. He sleeps alone in a hammock. To satisfy sexual desires, he and the wife of his choice enjoy the sanctuary of the corn shed in the distant family milpa. On their homeward trek, the wife trudges far behind her empty-handed husband, burdened with a fifty-pound load of unshelled corn, or an equal weight of mahogany firewood.

Old Chan K'in, with three wives, and eight

of fourteen children living with them, slept alone in a hammock. Under each end of the hammock stood a large, wide-mouthed clay pot. When the nights were rainy, and the wind blew cold, one of three wives remained awake throughout the night. It would be her turn to keep the clay pots filled to the brims with red-hot coals procured from the perpetually burning wood fire at one end of the large hut. The heat from the potted coals, wafting upward through the open-net hammock, kept the seventy-two-year-old Chan K'in warm and cozy throughout the chilly night hours. The old monarch also enjoyed this makeshift heating luxury on days when it was too cold and wet to work in the milpa, or sit in the open god house.

I asked Chan K'in if there was ever any dissension among his wives. He said yes. Did he intercede in these wifely squabbles? The answer was no. Did the wives ever quarrel over which one of them would walk to the milpa corn shed with him? The old fellow grinned, and said yes.

Sickness and disease are a commonplace way of life for the Lacandons. They are extremely susceptible to lung and respiratory ailments. During the many months of soaking, often cold rains, they are the constant victims of colds, infections, influenza, and pneumonia. The people are afflicted with many nonseasonal diseases and disorders. Prevalent among these are tuberculosis, typhoid, smallpox, amoebic dysentery, hookworms, intestinal and stomach worms, lung flukes, and other serious disorders.

Jorge suffered occasional epileptic seizures. A young woman who lived on the north side of the lake went into frenzied convulsions each time that an airplane landed at the airstrip. She would fall to the ground, where she would thrash her arms and legs wildly, and cry and scream until the plane taxied to a halt and the engine was stilled. She would lie on the ground and whimper until the pilot started the motor for the takeoff, and then relapse into convulsions until the airplane disappeared over the mountains.

Several of the women and children of the village exhibited symptoms of mental disorders. One young woman in particular suffered a form of personality disorder. She flew into periodical fits of uncontrolled rage during which she vented her outburst by beating her husband's dog. The poor beast lost one eye as the result of one beating. On another occasion, she nearly severed the dog's tail with a slash of her machete.

Governor Suarez attributed the nearly extinct status of the Lacandons primarily to the dreaded yellow fever, which apparently sweeps through the land in ten-year cycles. The Indians' peculiar

90

weakness and susceptibility to respiratory disease and infection has also been a major factor in their rapidly dwindling numbers. Tuberculosis, yellow fever, malaria, smallpox, and other killer diseases did not exist in the New World until the white man crossed the dividing seas to conquer, destroy, and pollute.

One of the governor's priority legislative programs during his tenure of office is organized and effective medical help, not only for the less than 150 Lacandons yet alive, but for the ultimate welfare of thousands upon thousands of other primitive peoples who form the major part of the population of Chiapas. Just a partial alleviation of the suffering from disease will require many years of sustained professional effort. Clinics must be established within reach of the widely scattered villages and settlements. Doctors and technicians must be persuaded to man these clinics. A continuing program of on-the-spot training of the Indians in hygiene, sanitation, and communicable disease control will be necessary. Of the many requirements for success, education of the primitive peoples must top the list. Well-meaning individuals should have a knowledge of the basic needs of the Indians before rushing in to give useless and even dangerous help.

One woman from the outside world had flown to Na'ha and delivered sufficient stocks of worm capsules, for example, to de-worm the village population several times over. In addition, she had brought large quantities of drug tablets for the treatment of dysentery. The medicines had been turned over to Chan K'in, Jr. with verbal instructions for dosages that he could not comprehend.

At Chan K'in's request, I inspected the medical supplies. Nearly all were useless because of deterioration. Several large glass containers labeled "For Dysentery Use" in large letters in fact contained worm capsules. Other vials, marked for worm treatment held dysentery tablets. Fortunately, the Lacandons had not used the medicines.

We had brought with us ample first aid supplies, and a large quantity of specific drugs and medicines recommended by Governor Suarez. I soon became concerned about our supply levels, for I was kept busy treating the sick, particularly the very young children. It was overall, a frustrating and mostly a single-handed effort. I received almost no support from the parents. It was not that they were callously indifferent or unfeeling about the sad plight of their children. They evidently appreciated my attempts to help, for they tried to do my bidding. The pain mirrored in their eyes told me that they indeed loved their children.

92

The following account is typical of the many medical situations that confronted me at Na'ha: A five-year-old girl, in a family of seven persons, was suffering from a severe chest cold that was bordering on pneumonia. Racked with a constant and painful cough and crying piteously, the small girl followed her mother's every footstep. The mother ignored her and impassively plodded on with her endless chores. There was nothing the poor woman could do for the sick child.

I offered to help the little girl. I could not communicate with the mother, but her smile was her consent. When I approached the girl to insert the clinical thermometer in her mouth, she recoiled in terror and clung to her mother's legs. I eventually calmed her and obtained the temperature reading. It was over 103 degrees. I led the child to her bare wooden pallet and covered her feverish body with a few dirty rags I found lying about in the incredibly filthy hut. I managed to convey to the mother that I wanted some oranges. She gathered several that had fallen from a nearby tree. I showed her how to squeeze the juice from an orange, and she half filled a dirty clay bowl and brought it to me. My little patient, no longer afraid of me, swallowed some antibiotic tablets, an aspirin, and all of the orange juice. I sat beside her until she fell asleep.

Before I left the hut the father came in. I told

him and his wife to give the girl another bowl of orange juice when she awakened. She was to have nothing to eat, but was to be encouraged to drink plenty of water. Further, she was not to leave her bed, and the other children were to stay away from her. They nodded with a smile to all of my requests, but I sincerely doubted that they had really understood any of them.

Four hours later I returned to give the child additional medication. The family was sitting in a tight circle around the fire. My patient sat with them with her bare bottom on the ground, and her skimpy skirt pulled tightly about her knees. She was coughing and heavy phlegm flowed from her nostrils. Between rasping coughs, she was taking small bites out of a huge tortilla and swallowing each morsel with a generous coating of germ laden mucous.

I scolded the father and mother for allowing the girl to leave her bed. They simply looked at me with their large brown eyes and smiled. I knew without asking that the little girl had received no more orange juice. I gave her another dose of medicine, a bowl of orange juice, and put her back in bed.

Early the next morning I saw my patient walking aimlessly about in the cold rain. I ran to her and led her by the hand into her hut. I administered another dose of medicine, and from habit rather than design, put her back in her bed. I gave up trying to make her ever-smiling parents understand what they could do to help their sick daughter recover. Later that morning the father came to our hut. He handed me three fresh eggs and left without a word.

The little girl recovered, but not until everybody in the family had fallen prey to the infectious illness. It was not until the month of March came with the drying, healing sunshine that the respiratory illnesses in the village subsided. I was thankful, for the precious drugs and medicines were almost totally expended.

Estelle, Jon, and I maintained our good health throughout our stay with the Lacandon. However, rarely can a person live in such an unhealthy environment for an extended period without paying a medical price of some kind. After we returned to the United States, Jon and I had to undergo extended treatment for serious amoebic disorders.

Every Lacandon is afflicted with worms and parasites of different types. The evidence of worm infestation was shocking to behold. An old woman was walking past our hut with a water-filled gourd in each hand. She was seized by a violent, choking cough. Retching and gagging, and struggling for breath, she disgorged an eight-inch-long worm from her mouth. Placing a gourd on the ground, she wiped the spittle from her pointed chin with the back of her hand. She picked up the water gourd and walked on as if nothing unusual had happened. On another day, we watched a man expel a long worm in the same manner, and with the same nonchalance.

My status as a medicine man grew apace, and my services were in constant demand. I successfully treated those illnesses for which I felt qualified. My heart ached for much more medical knowledge than I possess as I watched the Lacandons stoically suffer diseases which were beyond my capability to treat.

In the area of emergency medical care, I was kept busy. Most of the injuries were caused by the machete. Everybody except the babies owned one. It was disturbing to observe four- and five-year-old tots recklessly slicing the air with the wicked implement while at play. The gods must have been benevolent, for none of the little tykes were hurt. The older boys and the men at times became careless with the great knife and gashed themselves severely. The machete seldom inflicts a minor wound.

The Lacandons do very little to treat an injury, or an open wound. If the injury is in the area of the head, neck, or torso, they do nothing. Should the wound be located on an arm or a leg, they do not wash or cleanse the damaged area.

96

The only treatment consists of one layer of dirty cloth wrapped directly over the gashed tissue. The Lacandons appear to have an unusual resistance to infections resulting from cuts and injuries, and they heal very quickly.

Whether an injury is of a minor or major nature, the Lacandons follow a curious custom. Every person who sees an injury on any individual will run to his hut and get a length of cotton string which he will take back to the injured person and tie into a loose loop, which is placed as close to the wound as possible. If the damage is on an arm or hand, the string is looped around the wrist. Should a leg or foot be involved, the string loop is placed around the ankle. Should the wound be in an area of the torso, the string goes around the waist. Damage to the neck or the head causes the loop to go around the neck.

The purpose of the loop of string is to ward off the evil dwarfs who are the causes of all illness. We noted that some individuals, when peering at another person's injury, did not affix the customary loop of string. They merely spit upon the wound and walked away, chanting softly to the gods.

Incidentally, a baby receives the full string treatment at the moment of birth. Loops are tied around each ankle, the waist, both wrists, and the neck. The protections against the evil dwarfs

97

are left in place until the infant's severed umbilical has completely healed.

In February, Pepe Martinez flew in, bringing three passengers and their camping gear and equipment. Trudy Blom accompanied by a Dr. S. M. Tenny, of Hanover, New Hampshire, and his teen-aged son, were to spend a week in Trudy's camp. Dr. Tenny conducted a study of the Lacandons' respiratory systems. The examinations and measurements were made at the camp. Trudy, whom the Lacandons trust, asked them to report for examinations. They responded, reluctantly, coming to the camp each day, singly and in pairs from the north side of the lake, and from the village. The doctor and his son seldom came to the village. When we made our regular wash and bathday pilgrimages to the north side, we stopped at Trudy's camp for brief chats with the doctor and his son. Although we would miss not having a doctor available so near to us, the day of his departure was a red-letter day, for when Pepe flew in to pick up Trudy and her charges, he brought us a large bundle of mail from home.

By modern medical standards, the conditions under which a Lacandon woman gives birth to a baby are horrendous. There is, of course, no prenatal or postnatal care of any consequence. A pregnant woman accomplishes her daily work

98

routine without letup until the time for delivery. The baby is born in a small "birth hut," well removed from the family dwelling. The woman may be attended by one, sometimes two, midwives who have experienced childbirth. A husband is not permitted to witness the birth of his child. During his wife's ordeal he will be found in the god house, chanting to his gods and probably praying that the newborn will be a girl. The material rewards to be gained from the eventual sale of a girl will enhance his prestige and influence in the village.

Regardless of the sex of the newborn baby, the father will generally ignore it throughout its infancy and childhood. The care and rearing of an offspring is strictly the mother's responsibility; however, she will be given assistance from the older children.

There were two pregnancies evident when we arrived at Na'ha village. Both were in Mateo's family. One was his number one wife, a beautiful woman in her thirties who had given birth to eight previous children. The other pregnancy concerned a very pretty, fifteen-year-old daughter, named Chan Nuk. I asked when the births were expected. No one knew. They could only hazard a rough guess, and indicate that it would be soon. Pregnancy and birth are very natural events and time means absolutely nothing to a Lacandon woman.

Chan Nuk had no husband. She had been married to a frowsy-haired young man whom we called Fuzzy. Before he purchased Chan Nuk for his wife, Fuzzy had married her younger sister. Trouble between the two sister-wives quickly developed, and for quite logical reasons. When both girls lived with their parents, Chan Nuk, being the eldest, had complete authority over her younger sister, as decreed by tribal custom. After the sister became the wife of Fuzzy, she gave him permission to wed Chan Nuk. The status of authority and control was now changed, for the first wife has control over subsequent wives purchased by her husband. Chan Nuk and her sister clashed bitterly. Life became unbearable for poor Fuzzy. To restore peace and sanity to his household, he negotiated with Mateo, who agreed, for a price, to take Chan Nuk back into his fold. By this time, Chan Nuk was pregnant. Her father was happy. The gods willing, the baby would be a girl!

Thursday, February 24, closed on a memorable, and unforgettable event. In the early night the three of us, and little Ky'um, were relaxing around the fire in our hut. A rapid series of agonized screams stabbed the darkness and brought us to our feet in sudden alarm. Had a jaguar attacked the village? Ky'um ran swiftly out of the hut. He soon returned, looking re-

100

lieved. He said it was Chan Nuk who had scream-
ed. She was having her baby.

There was a long period of silence, and then
came more piteous screams. The anguished cries
of pain gradually diminished and faded away.
Ky'um bid us goodnight, and we went to bed,
our hearts heavy with concern for Chan Nuk.
We hoped that the poor girl's travail would end
quickly and safely for her and her newborn.

We were awakened by someone calling my
name from the front of the hut. I reached for my
flashlight. My watch indicated eleven o'clock. I
scrambled into my clothes, pulled on my boots,
and hurried outside. Young Chan K'in stood in
the pale moonlight. He said that Chan Nuk was
dying because she could not deliver her baby.
Would I help her? I reminded him of the taboo
that barred a man from attending a birth. He
said that Mateo was convinced that I could help
his daughter, and he had appealed to old Chan
K'in to ask for my assistance. The taboo had
been waived.

Desperate thoughts raced through my mind
as I weighed my decision. I mentally reviewed
what I knew about childbirth and delivery pro-
cedures. I was appalled at my ignorance. Lacking
expert knowledge, without any instruments —
nothing to work with but my bare hands, I wondered if I could be of any help to the stricken girl.

101

If she should actually die, would the Lacandons blame me? And if they did, what would be the ultimate fate of my beloved wife and son? The questions were many and potent. Yet, there was but one compelling, overall answer. I must try to help Chan Nuk.

Chan K'in, Jr. led me rapidly down the path to the tiny birth hut standing on the extreme southern boundary of the village clearing. He left me at the slatted door and walked to the god house where all of the men had congregated earlier. I sighed deeply, and looked pleadingly beyond the cold, impersonal stars, before removing the door slats and stepping inside the hut.

The eerie, grotesque setting of the dark interior would have awed the devil.

A small hammock drooped by the right wall of the windowless room. Two small, upright poles stood about four feet apart in the left center of the eight by ten feet floor area. A third pole, perhaps two inches in diameter, was secured horizontally to the uprights by strips of bark. The horizontal pole was about three feet above the dirt floor. At the base of each upright pole a small heap of mahogany pitch shavings were burning. The flames sputtered and choked in the acrid black smoke that enveloped the interior of the hut. The darting, yellow orange tongues of fire licked upward and cast weirdly dancing shadows about the room.

Clad in a wide skirt and loose-fitting blouse, barefooted Chan Nuk was squatted before the uprights with both hands clutching the horizontal pole. She was bent forward from the waist and her long black hair cascaded nearly to the ground. Every line and crease in her contorted face reflected her agony. Huge beads of perspiration rolled down her cheeks to pause and quiver on her chin before dropping to the ground.

A silent, stony-faced woman sat cross-legged and unmoving in front of the girl. Another woman supported Chan Nuk and strained to keep the moaning, exhausted girl upright in the squatting position. Outside of the hut there was a confusing crescendo of swirling sounds. Night birds and animals were crying, screaming, and whistling. Millions of insects, plus tree toads and lake frogs competed lustily for decibel space. An incessant chorus of chanting men came from the god house, as they implored the gods for good favor in this critical moment in Chan Nuk's life. Penetrating above the uproar that came from the god house was the wailing, nonstop chant of Mateo.

The phlegmatic woman sitting in front of Chan Nuk held my flashlight as I examined the girl. I was greatly relieved to find the baby in the normal birth position. There at least would not be the peril attendent upon a breech birth. I could not determine if the baby was alive. I feared that it might be stillborn.

Chan Nuk's major difficulty soon became evident. She was small-structured, and the baby was much too large. Without proper assistance, she could not deliver. There was no way that I could grasp the baby with my hands and help Chan Nuk. An alternate possible solution came to my mind. I positioned myself behind the girl with my left knee on the ground. I placed my right knee in the center of her lower back area. I then encircled my arms around her body at the hip-line and clasped my left wrist with my right hand.

I established an inward and downward rhythmic compression over her lower abdominal area, applying as much pressure as I thought was safe. Chan Nuk responded weakly, and I timed my efforts with her faint contractions. Only once did the girl indicate that I was hurting her. There were no words, no outcry. She touched my hands and pushed them gently downward to a less painful position on her abdomen.

I continued the rhythmic, heavy pressure. The pain-wracked girl gripped the cross bar and arched her straining body backward, resting her head on my shoulder. Her cheek was pressed to mine and our sweat intermingled and soaked our clothing. The two impassive women sat cross-legged in front of us, silent and staring. During the desperate drama I lost all sense of time, and almost of reason. I asked myself what I was doing there. Was I really involved, or was I playing a role in an awful nightmare?

The acrid black smoke from the burning piles of pitch hurt my eyes and lungs. Biting fleas were driving me to distraction, but I could not release Chan Nuk and dislodge my tormentors. I was nearing the point of exhaustion, and poor Chan Nuk was beyond further ability to carry on. Then the eternal miracle of birth happened. I heard the slight thump when the baby struck the blood-soaked earth. It lay on its back in a lifeless, spread-eagled position. Chan Nuk groaned feebly and went limp in my arms. I continued to hold her as I gazed at the motionless baby boy. He lay inert for what seemed an eternity, and I thought the baby was surely dead.

A sudden convulsion jerked the infant's glistening, copper brown body. The tiny fingers twitched, and the baby emitted a strangled, plaintive wail. The beautiful sound was like music to my ears. As soon as the baby cried out, the two women got busy. I continued to hold the still limp Chan Nuk and watched, for I wanted to learn what they would do without my help or interference.

105

The women first tied loops of string around the newborn's ankles, waist, wrists, and neck. The evil dwarfs thusly thwarted, the women then tied a length of cotton string tightly around the baby's umbilical cord. One of the women produced a short length of carisa fiber from which she pulled a narrow strip, using only her thumb and forefinger. The edges of the carisa strip were razor sharp. Holding the strip tautly by each end, the woman used its sharp edge to cleanly sever the umbilical cord. Here was another graphic demonstration of native wisdom and ingenuity. She had not touched the cutting edge of the fiber strip before using it to cut the cord. Nature had provided an instrument that presented far less chance of infection than would the use of a piece of metal, or the edge of a machete blade.

The expulsion of the placenta was uncomplicated. Chan Nuk was badly torn. I could have sterilized sewing thread and a needle by boiling water, and sutured the most serious rips, but since there was no uncontrollable hemorrhaging, I decided against it. I placed the spent young mother in the hammock. One of the women wrapped the baby in a piece of dirty cloth before placing him in the hammock with Chan Nuk.

At last it was all over. The sphinxlike woman followed me to the door of the hut. Her leathery face creased into a smile, and she gently touched my shoulder with her hand as I removed the door slats. I understood and deeply appreciated the silent gesture of gratitude.

On the way to my hut, I stopped briefly on the pathway and let the cool, fresh air cleanse the pitch smoke from my parched lungs and soothe my burning eyes. The god house was empty. The men had stopped their chanting almost at the moment of the baby's birth. The gods had answered the Lacandons' prayers. I lifted my eyes skyward toward the star-dusted boulevard of the Milky Way gleaming across the velvety heavens, and thanked the God in whom I believe for answering mine.

My family was waiting for me, wide awake and hungering for news. Jon had thoughtfully prepared hot coffee. Over several cups of the relaxing brew I recounted what had transpired during my more than two hours of absence. When we finally went to bed, I could not sleep. Estelle tossed and turned also, but for reasons quite different from mine. I had brought some of Chan Nuk's fleas to bed, and they had quickly transferred to my wife's sweeter, more tender pastures.

At sunrise, Mateo and Chan Nuk's mother appeared at our doorway. She was holding two small, crudely made clay dolls, which represented a Lacandon man and woman. The dolls were dressed in typical Lacandon costumes. Tears filmed Mateo's eyes as he awkwardly thanked me for attending Chan Nuk. He presented me with the dolls and walked swiftly away. The woman smiled shyly, and followed her husband down the path.

After our breakfast, Estelle, Jon, and I visited Chan Nuk. She had moved from the birth hut to the family dwelling. We found her sitting cross-legged on a pallet with her baby on her lap. She smiled weakly at us, then lowered her head and stroked the sleeping infant's shock of black hair. She and the baby appeared to be in good condition. Other than giving Chan Nuk two antibiotic tablets, there was nothing for me to do.

I led Estelle and Jon to the birth hut. The interior was much as it had been when I left the night before. Nothing had been moved, or cleaned. A fetid odor permeated the hut. The blood-soaked earth below the horizontal pole had dried and was buzzing with scavenging flies. We lingered in the chamber of horrors only long enough to obtain some photographs.

Following the Lacandons' normal postnatal custom, Chan Nuk remained secluded in her hut, recuperating, and caring for her newborn son. I looked in on her daily, and was surprised at her rapid recovery. On the fourth day, she resumed her usual work routine. It was on this day that she gave the baby his first cleansing, using plain water and a rag.

On the fifth day after the baby's birth, the gods were called to come and drink sacred posol with the women of the village. Posol is a regularly consumed semi-liquid food made from ground corn mixed with water. However, when prepared in the set-apart holy kitchen, the posol becomes sacred. The posol drinking ceremony is not conducted at the god house. Women are considered as unclean and are barred therefrom. The posol rites are held in the sacred kitchen, which is reserved strictly for the women. Before partaking of the sacred posol, the women must wash their hands. In the unlikely event that a woman has washed her skirt or blouse on the day of the ceremony, she is not allowed to participate.

The new baby was not named at birth. Weeks, months, perhaps years would go by before it would officially be named. A few days after the birth of the baby, Mateo confided to me that his new grandson would eventually bear the name of Chan K'in!

I looked in on Chan Nuk regularly for the first ten days after the baby's birth, in the event that she or the little one developed complications, especially infection. Both progressed satisfactorily. Chan Nuk, a really beautiful girl, was extremely proud of her first-born, and cared for him with tender devotion. On one of my visits I watched as she rubbed the baby's body with a whole plant leaf. Called *eehar'ik* by the Lacandon, the leaf contains properties that prevent the outbreak of rash on a baby's sensitive skin. Incidently, Fuzzy, the baby's father, never visited the baby. He ignored it, and Chan Nuk, completely.

CHAPTER 4

The last days of February were the beginning of the good weather season. The cold and wet storms from the north ceased their frequent onslaughts and were replaced by soft tropical breez-

111

es coming from Guatemala. Daytime skies were a deep blue, flecked with lazily drifting white clouds, and the hot sun warmed the darkly shaded floor of the jungle. Our bath and washday journeys to the north side of the lake became easier and more enjoyable as the deep mire of the trail dried.

Except for the biting fleas, gnats, and mosquitos, our daily life became almost idyllic. We had made our hut as functional and comfortable as circumstances and facilities permitted. Dry, seasoned mahogany firewood became easy to locate. Jon and I spent one day each week laying in a supply of the wood. As we cut and splintered the beautifully grained mahogany from a wind-fallen tree, I sometimes wondered what the wood might be worth by the board foot at a stateside lumberyard.

Unlike the Lacandons, who maintain their fires constantly, we allowed ours to burn out every night before going to bed. I arose every morning before dawn. My first and least pleasant task was starting the breakfast fire. I held a match to a small heap of shavings, and when they were burning steadily, I added larger pieces of wood, which never burned properly until I blew myself dizzy fanning the stubborn flames.

One morning as I was having my usual difficulty in starting the breakfast fire, Ky'um came

112

in and watched me trying to blow life into the feeble flames. He left, and returned with a chunk of almost solid pitch that weighed about twenty pounds. He used my hunting knife to slice a few thin slivers from the piece of pitch and added them to the stock of wood in the fireplace. Within twenty minutes a glowing bed of perfect cooking coals was formed.

I thanked Ky'um for his help and returned the chunk of pitch to him. He refused to take it. He had brought it as a gift. Because of the little fellow's thoughtfulness, the chore of starting a fire would no longer be an onerous task.

I prepared breakfast each morning before rousting my two sleepyheads out of their sleeping bags. After cleaning the breakfast utensils we went about our self-appointed assignments for the day. Each of us knew the importance of keeping a detailed journal of all that we learned, and when taking photographs, to make every picture tell a story.

Our complete acceptance by the Lacandons came about after I helped deliver Chan Nuk's baby. Those who had ignored and avoided us became open and friendly. We were made to feel as though we were regular members of the village. When I was not involved with Chan K'in, Jr. in a study of the Maya gods and the language, I spent as much time as I could with

113

his father, Chan K'in. Since the old fellow divided his daytime activities between his distant milpa and the god house, our meetings usually took place at his hut in the late evening.

I developed a deep affection and respect for Chan K'in. He showed his regard for me by the frequent gifts of cigars, bundles of cured tobacco leaves, eggs, and portions of cooked foods such as tortillas and boiled cuts of wild game. There was little I could present to him other than cigarettes and occasionally a sample of our food.

Chan K'in had once remarked that he admired my pipe, and had always wanted to own one. In fact, he had attempted to make a pipe from clay, but it crumbled into bits the first time he tried to stuff the bowl with tobacco. On a subsequent visit with him I brought with me my spare briar pipe. After we were seated about the fire, I filled the pipe with tobacco, lighted it, and handed it to Chan K'in. He tried a few experimental puffs, grinned and nodded his appreciation, and settled back in his hammock for a wordless half-hour of serious smoking.

When I said good-night and started for the door, Chan K'in arose from his hammock and gave me the pipe. He thought that I had loaned it to him for an evening's enjoyment. When I finally convinced him that I had indeed given him the pipe to keep, the old man was over-

114

joyed. He and one of his wives came to our hut
the following day. Chan K'in presented me with
a large bundle of tobacco leaves neatly bound
with bark strips. His wife gave Estelle three
freshly laid hen eggs that were still warm to the
touch. I was both thrilled and touched when
Chan K'in, for the first time, expressed his feelings toward me in words. He said, "You are a
very good friend — very good!"

Chan K'in's weathered and wrinkled face
was as inscrutable as a Chinese Buddhist's stat-
ue; however he was a warm and gentle man,
beloved by everyone. He displayed a keen wisdom and when he spoke, those about him listened intently. Many of the Lacandons considered
Chan K'in to be a direct descendant of the Maya
gods. His knowledge of the gods and their ways
was apparently limitless and all came to him for
advice and instruction in religious matters. He
had taught his son Chan K'in well. One day,
the young man would assume the unofficial, but
undisputed role as the spiritual and moral leader
of the people at Na'ha. The old man was also
grooming little Ky'um for leadership duties in
the event the eldest son could not, or would not,
carry on after the father's death.

Although no actual birthdate was known,
Chan K'in was about seventy-two years of age.
He was born in Saka'tona, a Lacandon village

that ceased to function many years ago. Chan K'in told me that when he was a very young man, with a wife, federal soldiers came to the jungles to search out and destroy the Lacandon people. After the initial surprise onslaughts in which many were killed, the Lacandons fled deep into the jungle interior and lived a nomadic life of constant terror. Chan K'in recalled that he and his wife lived in the jungles like hunted animals, ever on the move, and hiding in crude shelters and mountain caves, lest they be found by the soldiers and shot to death. Chan K'in insisted that he never learned why the Lacandons were so viciously persecuted.

Chan K'in had known Carlos Frey, an American draft evader who fled the United States during the closing stages of World War II, and disappeared in the Selva Lacandon, where he was to become a legend. He was the first white man to be completely adopted into the Lacandon culture. He learned the language, married a Lacandon maiden, and became to all intents and purposes a genuine member of the tribe.

Frey expressed a great interest in the Maya religion and the Lacandons were more than happy to teach him what they knew. On one occasion, Frey was privileged to accompany a group of men on a worship pilgrimage to the hidden ruins of Bonampak. Although he had chosen the

116

Lacandon way of life to the exclusion of civilization's interests, Frey sensed a golden opportunity for fame and fortune when he gazed at the painted murals on the walls of a temple at Bonampak.

Frey left the Lacandons for a short time and returned to the outside world to seek the support necessary to capitalize on his treasure find. He was rebuffed. He returned to Chiapas, where he met Giles Healey, a photographer, whom he led to the Bonampak ruins. Carlos Frey was, ironically, to be rebuffed again. The photographs of the Mayan murals brought Healey the honor of being the discoverer of Bonampak.

Dame Fate dealt Carlos Frey one final blow. In 1955, Frey reportedly jumped from a dugout canoe in a vain attempt to save a nonswimmer companion who had fallen overboard. Accordingly to generally accepted reports, both men drowned.

In addition to Chan K'in, there were other men at Na'ha who had known Carlos Frey. My first inquiries into the details of his death brought furtive glances, but no answers. Before we left Na'ha, I was informed that Carlos Frey had not drowned. He had once fought a Lacandon over the favors of a woman. The defeated Indian had sworn to exact vengeance. On that fateful day on the river, Carlos Frey did indeed disappear

117

in the swirling waters, not from drowning, but with a bullet in his brain.

The start of the good weather season in February was also the beginning of a busy time for those Lacandons who would have to wrest new milpas from the stubborn jungle to replace the corn fields that were no longer capable of producing corn. The new fields had to be ready for planting by the first part of April, when the ground would be sufficiently dry to germinate the new seed corn.

Several of the families needed to replace their milpas. In the race against time, the families involved would bestir themselves while it was yet dark. By the time the sun had dispelled the mists of dawn, the village was almost deserted. Some of the fields were nearby. Others were long distances from the village. Chan K'in's milpa was about three miles to the south, on the slope of a mountain valley.

The Lacandons' primitive methods of clearing a field in the jungle, planting, harvesting, and storing the corn, date back into antiquity. Perhaps the only "new" thing in the milpa clearing process is the machete. An all-purpose cutting implement and weapon, the machete is used by most natives of Central, and South America.

118

Without it, the Lacandons would indeed be in an almost hopeless situation.

The most important factor in selecting a new milpa site is the location. This is determined by several critical factors: the thickness of the underbrush, the lushness of the overall native vegetation, and the number and size of the trees. The terrain must have sufficient natural drainage, and the soil must be of the type and depth most suited to the growing of corn. After the site selection, the area has to be cleared. All in the family who can wield a machete go to work.

Chan K'in's milpa was over three years old and had served its useful purpose. The old man decided to clear a new field adjacent to the worn-out one. Jon and I spent an entire day observing and photographing Chan K'in, his three wives, and a six-year-old son, hack and slash at the mass of jungle. The brush and ground cover were cut down first. Then followed the larger bushes, and smaller trees. The cuttings were not piled, but were left lying where they fell. The large trees that were in the area required a special method to cut down. And, it takes several days of extremely hard and dangerous work as some of the trees were one hundred feet in height, and three or four feet in base diameter.

The Lacandons first erect a flimsy pole scaffold that extends about ten feet above the flared

119

base of the tree. A man stands on the swaying platform and hacks away with a machete until the towering giant crashes to earth.

Chan K'in's youngest wife had brought her eight-week-old baby with her. She carried the infant on her back in a length of cloth looped over her shoulder and neck. As she vigorously swung her machete in long arching strokes, the curled-up baby swung back and forth like a pendulum. After a time, the infant began to cry and wriggle in discomfort. The young mother tied the suspension cloth between two small saplings where it formed a small hammock. She gave the baby one of her breasts, and when it had sucked its fill of milk, she placed it in the hammock and returned to her labors. Although the cloth hammock was freshly soaked with urine, and gnats and flies covered the baby's face, the little one lay quiet and content.

The Lacandons toiled all morning, stopping once to eat posol, a thick liquid of ground corn and water. During the hot day, the workers frequently drank a beverage of peppers and water. The peppers, native to the land, resemble the red pod pepper commonly known the world over; however, this specie is much hotter. So much hotter, in fact, that the Lacandons cannot eat them. The drink recipe is simple. About twelve hours before the women go to the milpa,

120

they drop two or three of the pepper pods in a gourd full of water. The result is a throat-burning but satisfying drink.

In midafternoon, when the searing sun and the biting gnats had combined to produce maximum human discomfort, the Indians stopped working and prepared to return home. They went to the corn shed that stood at one end of the old milpa, where the remainder of the previous season's corn was stored. Chan K'in sat and rested in the shade of the shed while each of his wives filled a large, loosely woven fiber bag to capacity with ears of unhusked corn. The filled bags weighed about eighty pounds each.

Chan K'in did not give his wives an opportunity to rest. When they finished filling the bags, he arose and started down the trail to the village. Save for his machete, he was empty-handed. The wives helped each other to their feet with the tremendous loads of corn and trotted after him, bending forward at the waist to counter-balance the pressure exerted on their foreheads by the bark strip tumplines. In addition to the load of corn, the young mother carried her baby in the cloth sling.

When the brush, vegetation, and trees have been leveled in the new milpa, the cuttings are left to dry. In late March the dried debris and fallen trees are set afire. The fires are maintained

121

until all that can burn is consumed. The large tree trunks, being green and unseasoned do not burn completely. They are left intact, and corn will be planted around them.

Planting time arrives in April. The seed corn is carried in a bag slung from the shoulder of the planter. A shallow hole is punched in the soft earth with a pointed stick. Five or six kernels of corn are dropped into the hole, which is then covered by stepping on it. With the next step forward the planting sequence is repeated. Unburned logs, large poles, and stumps preclude the planting of corn in rows. In addition to corn, the milpa is used to grow black beans, native squash, pumpkins, and gourds. Native tobacco is also raised in the milpa.

The milpa is not weeded or cultivated. The corn and other food plants are left to fend for themselves. The secondary crops are harvested as they mature. Beans are stored in the village huts, while pumpkins, squash, and gourds are left at the milpa, stacked beneath the overhanging thatched eaves of the corn storage shed.

When the corn has ripened the Lacandon women walk through the field and break each stalk bearing an ear of corn, causing the ear to hang with its top down. In this inverted position the rain cannot enter the covering husk and bring mildew and rot to the corn. The ears of corn,

122

with the husks left intact, are later harvested and stacked neatly in the storage shed. The husks continue to serve as natural raincoats, and also as quite effective barriers against would-be invader insects. The ears of corn are removed from storage only in the amount needed. Shelled by hand, the kernels are removed from the cob by pushing them against the rasping surface of an empty cob.

The Lacandons augment their primarily corn and vegetable diet with the meat of wild game, and the natural foods provided by the tropical environment. These include bananas, plantains, mangoes, guavas, papayas, berries, etc. The Indians are especially fond of a sweet yam which is native to the area. As previously mentioned, orange trees grow within the village limits, but the bulk of the healthful fruit is allowed to go to waste. A pear-shaped fruit of the sapadillo, or chicle tree, is prized for its sweet, candylike flavor. The resin of the sapadillo provides raw, flavorless chewing gum for the children.

The source of calcium in the Lacandons' diet is obtained from snail shells. The women gather large amounts of snails from the shallow and reedy sections of the lake. The meat is picked from the shells with a small sharpened stick, and is eaten raw, on the spot. At nightfall, the shells are heaped in the coals of the fireplace. The next

123

morning, a mound of gray calcium ash is removed, to be used in the daily preparation of tortillas. The snail shell ash is added to the unground corn in a ratio of one handful to approximately a half-bushel of corn.

The tobacco leaves are harvested and hung in a small curing shed at the milpa. When cured, the leaves are fashioned and tied with strips of bark into bundles weighing about three pounds each. The bundles are stored in the dwelling of the owner. Cigars are hand-rolled by the women. Their saliva serves as the adhesive ingredient to hold the cigar leaves together.

Every Lacandon, except the infants, smoke cigars. Two-year-old youngsters puffed on big cigars as naturally, and with as much evident enjoyment, as children of our land suck on a lollipop. The women carried an extra cigar tied to their single braid of hair. Quite often the spare cigar was no more than a previously smoked and well-chewed butt.

We gained no evidence that the Lacandons of Na'ha use drugs of any kind, although reportedly, the ones at Lake Memsa'bok do so to excess. The greatest part of the blame for drug abuse there, as well as among other Indian tribes of Chiapas, lies with unprincipled, wandering hippies from the United States.

It is reasonable to assume that the Lacandons

of Na'ha use certain herbs for medicinal purposes, but we learned of only one plant so used. The manner in which we learned of this particular herb was rather humorous. Ky'um pointed out a clump of long, narrow-bladed grass that was growing in front of our hut. He said that when brewed, the pale-green grass made an excellent drink. We brought a pan of water to a boil. Ky'um tied about six of the narrow grass blades into a loose knot, and dropped it into the boiling water. After about five minutes, he removed the pan from the fire, then the knot of limply boiled grass blades from the now-yellowed water. The drink was ready. It had a distinct lemon flavor, and we found it to be a refreshing and satisfying beverage. We drank it often and suffered no ill aftereffects. Just before we left Na'ha, we learned that the lemon grass "tea" was used by the Lacandons as a medicine. Supposedly, it eased severe gastric disturbances, and also pacified stomach and intestinal worms.

Before leaving the United States, I had received written permission from Mexican authorities to take with us a 30.06 caliber game rifle, a .22 caliber rifle, and a limited amount of ammunition for each weapon. I wanted the guns for emergency protective measures that might well arise, and also to perhaps influence the La-

125

candons in our behalf by procuring wild game for them.

Enroute to Chiapas I had learned that the federal government prohibited the sale or purchase by any one of any type of ammunition, including .22 caliber cartridges. This drastic and fully enforced measure had been enacted into law because of the threat of terrorist activities by political extremists, many of whom filter into Mexico from neighboring Latin-American countries. From a national security standpoint, the edict was probably necessary. But it dealt a crushing blow to the thousands of primitive peoples who rely on the simple .22 rifle as their principal means of obtaining vital meat supplies.

The Lacandons no longer hunt with the bow and stone-tipped arrows. These implements of the hunt were replaced long ago with the .22 rifle. There were five such weapons in Na'ha village. Two of the guns were in reasonably safe condition. The others were deteriorated, single-shot antiques that posed more of a lethal threat to the shooter than to the intended target.

The Lacandons had no ammunition for the guns, and of course, could not obtain any. They hunted game every day that the weather permitted, using machetes and dogs, and usually returning to the village empty-handed and very discouraged. Our work schedule, plus other cir-

126

cumstances, did not permit me to hunt for the Lacandons as I had intended. I decided that the best solution would be to parcel out the 500 rounds of .22 caliber cartridges to the men who owned the rifles, and let them shoot their own game.

I also changed my mind about keeping my rifles at Na'ha. We were no longer concerned about our personal safety in the village, for the Lacandons had become friends whom we could trust. Pepe Martinez flew in one day and I prevailed upon him to take the guns to San Cristobal, and leave them in care of Señor Zebadua. I was greatly relieved when the weapons were gone. I was free from the nagging worry of losing the guns to roving guerrillas who might appear in the village, a possibility I had been officially warned could happen. I was also rid of the time consuming task of maintaining the rifles in a rust-free and operable condition.

The meat-starved people were jubilant when I began to distribute the .22 ammunition. I did not give all of the cartridges away at one time, but rationed them to the five rifle owners at the rate of five rounds per man, per week. The hunters were ultra-conservative with the scanty allowances, taking no more than two rounds with them on a hunt. The Lacandons' shooting skills were remarkable. They always returned to

127

the village with game, and usually with only one cartridge expended.

A wide variety of game was killed by the hunters. Game birds included parrots, macaws, toucans, doves, and turkeys. Among the animals bagged were deer, peccary, tapir, agouti, and teposquintl. Monkeys are highly prized for their meat, but are few in number. The last outbreak of yellow fever in the Na'ha region almost wiped them out.

The teposquintl was the easiest animal for the Lacandons to hunt. Before I gave them ammunition for their rifles, the men sometimes ran one of the animals down with dogs, and killed it with a machete. The teposquintl is a member of the rodent family. When skinned, it looked like the carcass of a suckling pig. Those brought in by hunters weighed from ten to thirty pounds. Short haired, light brown in color, the animal has silver stripes on its back. It has a ratlike face and very sharp, spadelike front teeth. The hind legs are considerably longer than the front ones, and the feet are large and armed with heavy black claws. The tail is long, tapered, and hairless. The teposquintl subsists on berries, roots, acorns, etc.

At least one man, with his dog, went hunting every day that weather conditions permitted. If the hunt proved successful, the game was skinned, washed in the muddy water of the

128

stream by our hut, cut into pieces, and boiled by the hunter's wife, or wives. The cooked meat was shared with the other village families. My family was usually included. Jon is a strict vegetarian, and Estelle would not eat the native-cooked meat, fearing that it would be a piece of teposquintl rat. In the interest of research, I ate at least one bite of each species of bird and animal cooked by the Lacandon and given to us. The samples were invariably good to the taste. We never threw away uneaten food, whether ours, or the Indians' variety, but gave the left-overs to the always hungry children.

CHAPTER 5

During the height of the
Maya classical period
there were at least twelve
major gods, and a host
of minor deities. The major gods were mortal.
Some of the minor gods were also mortal, while

131

others were certain animals, birds, plants, and trees. At the end of the Maya civilization there existed hundreds, perhaps thousands, of lesser gods. It is quite conceivable that the ever burgeoning god structure became more than the supporting peasant populace could bear, thus contributing to the rapid fall and disappearance of the mighty empire.

Chan K'in, Jr. was pleased that I wanted to learn as much as possible about the Lacandon god structure. To this end, he devoted many hours of painstaking and detailed instruction. I admired, and was grateful for, the young man's extreme patience with me, especially since tolerance was not one of his virtues. The following account contains many gaps that I was unable to fill, principally due to the communications barrier.

The Lacandons recognize nine major gods. I did not learn the number of minor deities, but there are many. I also did not learn the names and functions of the individual major gods, except for Hachak'yum, the chief god; a brother named Sukuk'yum; the god of the underworld, who is called Ky'sin, and who had once been a respected member of the major god assembly; and Itz'anoh'ku, a rain god who lived at Lake Itz'-anoh'ku, where his likeness, carved in a rock, remains to this day.

The story of the creation of the underworld, and the subsequent installation of Ky'sin as its ruling god, strangely parallels the biblical account of the rebel angel Lucifer, his fall from Heavenly grace, and his banishment to the place called Hell.

Long, long ago, the Maya gods lived at Palenque. Their homes were located at the top of the pyramids. Ky'sin, wickedly ambitious, wanted to become the chief god. He plotted to kill Hachak'yum, who was supreme over all. One day, as Ky'sin was walking near the base of Hachak'yum's pyramid, he looked up and saw the chief god standing alone on the top step. Ky'sin noted that there was nobody else around. This was the opportunity that he had been waiting for.

He quickly fitted an arrow to his bow, aimed at Hachak'yum, and loosed the string. The arrow sped true to its mark. Hachak'yum tumbled and rolled down the many steep steps of the pyramid and landed at Ky'sin's feet. He was not quite dead. Ky'sin strangled the remaining life from Hachak'yum, and cut off his head. He left the scene to prepare to assume the undisputed leadership of the gods.

Tupe, a son of Hachak'yum, found his father lying headless at the bottom of the pyramid. He was weeping over his dead father, when

Hachak'yum's voice said, "Tupe, my son, put my head where it belongs." Tupe replaced his father's head, but he put it on backward. His father told him to do it correctly. On the third attempt, the boy placed the head on in proper position.

Hachak'yum swore that he would punish Ky'sin severely for his evil schemes and ambitions. He created a body that looked exactly like himself, and left it lying, beheaded, at the base of the pyramid. He directed Tupe to behave as though the body was really that of his father, and to announce the death of the chief god. The supposed body of Hachak'yum was buried beneath the floor of his house, as was the custom in the case of a deceased god. All of the people went into a period of mourning for their beloved, former chief god, and Tupe sat by the tomb for four days with food for the supposedly departed leader. After the traditional four days of mourning, all of the gods and the people left Palenque, to live in the temple city of Yaxchilan.

During the period of mourning, Hachak'-yum had gone into the bowels of the earth to prepare a place for Ky'sin. On the fifth day, Ky'sin's house in the underworld was completed. Hachak'yum then caused a terrible earthquake to occur. The earth opened wide, and Ky'sin fell into the underworld, where Hachak'-

yum was waiting for him. He told Ky'sin that, because he was evil, and had tried to kill him, he (Ky'sin) was henceforth banished from the upper world, and must forever remain as the god of the underworld.

The wise Hachak'yum realized that merely leaving the incurably evil Ky'sin alone in the underworld domain would not prevent him from eventually destroying the world and eating all of the people. There would have to be some sort of firm and absolute control maintained over Ky'sin's activities. Hachak'yum returned to the upper world and went to Yaxchilan. He approached his brother, Sukuk'yum, who was one of the major gods, and asked him if he would consent to live in the underworld, and maintain control over the dreaded Ky'sin. Sukuk'yum agreed. Hachak'yum returned to the underworld and built a house for his brother. When it was finished, Sukuk'yum moved in, to also live in the underworld forever.

Under the ever watchful eye of Sukuk'yum, Ky'sin can never succeed in his determination to destroy the world. On occasion, he is permitted to create a small earthquake, or a volcanic eruption that is not too violent and destructive. Now and then, Sukuk'yum allows Ky'sin to eat a few people.

Since the day of his banishment to the underworld, Ky'sin has been the Lacandon symbol of all that is evil. Natural disasters such as earth-quakes, tidal waves, volcanoes, hurricanes, etc., are blamed upon him. Death, sickness, and all of mankind's miseries and misfortunes can be traced to Ky'sin's satanic influence. Solar and lunar eclipses are attempts by Ky'sin to destroy the world.

After the installation of Ky'sin as the god of the underworld, Hachak'yum returned to the upper world, and spent the remainder of his long life in Yaxchilan with his son Tupe, and a daughter named Kure.

In addition to protecting the world and the people from the fierce Ky'sin, Sukuk'yum takes care of the sun and the moon. Although both are very sacred, neither the sun nor the moon is considered a god, or a goddess. When not on their respective rounds in the heavens, K'in, the sun, and Ak'na, the moon, reside in the house of Sukuk'yum.

Each morning, Sukuk'yum places K'in in the proper position in the eastern sky. He points K'in's face westward, releases him, and bids him go. At dusk, after K'in has dipped below the western horizon, Sukuk'yum retrieves him and brings him to his home. He feeds him a dinner of peanuts, turkey, and other delicacies before putting him to bed for sleep and rest. Each eve-

136

ning, and every morning, Sukuk'yum provides the same guidance and care for Ak'na, the moon. There is a reason for Sukuk'yum's solicitous concern for K'in and Ak'na. Both are totally blind.

The Lacandons have a great and genuine fear of the underworld and do not like to talk of its horrors. All of them must go to this hell after death, where they must overcome many terrible obstacles before they can escape to the eternal rest and peace they will find in the blissful land of their gods. Those who fail to pass through the underworld will be devoured, and their lost souls will hopelessly and forever cry for deliverance from the terror and darkness of Ky'sin's domain.

When a Lacandon man dies, his body is placed in a hammock. Several small animal bones are put in one of his hands, and a lock of hair in the other. (I did not learn the significance of the lock of hair.) The corpse's mouth is filled with kernels of corn. The body is buried in the earth, and for a period of four days food is brought to the grave. The food will sustain the deceased during his perilous journey through the underworld. After the fourth day, the mourners return to their normal activities, and the grave site is never visited again.

On his route through the underworld, the

man paddles a dugout canoe across a wide expanse of turbulent and treacherous waters. Hideous and ravenous beasts lie in ambush along the way. When they attack, the Lacandon throws to them the bones he held in his hand. While the ferocious creatures fight over the bits of bones, he escapes. He will next be challenged by monstrous man-eating birds. The kernels of corn he carried in his mouth are utilized to feed and distract the demon birds, while he makes his way to the safety of the opposite shore, which is the gateway to the land of the gods.

A man who disobeyed the gods, or committed a serious crime during his lifetime, is doomed to remain in the underworld forever. The Lacandons also believe that the soul of a dog is necessary to escort them safely through the vast and trackless underworld. This belief makes it imperative that every Lacandon man own a dog.

If a dog is intentionally killed or injured by its master, the owner can never cross the Styxlike waters of the underworld. This belief was illustrated to us. A diseased and dying dog was permitted to suffer many agonizing days without care. The animal was tied to a stake near the owner's hut. Day and night, we listened to the poor beast's pitiful cries and low moans. In desperation we asked Chan K'in why the suffering dog was not put out of its misery. The old man

138

explained the religious reasons that prohibited such action. We argued that the mercy slaying of an incurably ill dog would be different from killing a healthy one in anger. Chan K'in shook his head in a vigorous denial, and we let the matter drop.

A dog is not killed at the death of its owner. The animal's soul is freed to go with his dead master. When the dog eventually dies, by whatever means, it will reunite with its soul, and his master, in the land of the gods.

Evidently, the burial methods, the trials of the underworld, and the need to own a dog, apply only to the men. A woman's fate after death was not explained. Women are not prohibited from, or punished for, the wilful mistreatment or killing of a dog. One young wife became angered at her husband's dog for no apparent reason and beat the animal into a senseless hulk with a club. Another woman, incensed at a dog that had stolen a tortilla from her kitchen, grabbed her machete. The fleeing thief was indeed fortunate that only its tail was sliced off.

The ancestors of the Lacandons worshipped their Maya gods in the magnificent ceremonial centers of Palenque, Yaxchilan, Bonampak, and others. When the remarkable Maya civilization perished, as all civilizations must, the Lacandons and their gods survived. The intervening centuries have mellowed both. The Lacandons are no longer the fierce warriors who unflinchingly obeyed the bloodthirsty whims of the once-demanding gods. No more are hearts torn from human breasts and while still pulsating, held aloft in triumph to the approving gods. Young virgins are no longer thrown alive into sacrificial pools of deep, black water. The Lacandons of today do not know that their ancestors once cut and mutilated their own tongues, fingers, and genitals, in order to obtain blood offerings for the gods.

There have been important changes, and much has been forgotten, but the Lacandon life of today still revolves around their gods. Almost nothing is planned or attempted without first consulting with their deities in a primitive god house setting that replaces the splendorous temples of the past. The sacred god house was located on the eastern limits of the village, set well apart from the dwellings.

The god house consisted of an open-sided, palm-roofed shelter that measured approximately twenty by thirty feet in dimension. The main entrance faced to the east. Immediately inside the entrance were nine oddly shaped stools. The rectangular seats were concave, twenty by fourteen inches in size and one inch thick. Each stool,

140

with its four short, pyramid-shaped legs, had been carved in one piece from a section of a mahogany log. The tops of the stools were beautifully polished from many years of regular usage.

At each end of the god house was a fireplace. Three stones placed in a triangle formed the fire site, with one stone pointing to the east. Two wide-meshed fiber nets, filled with small gourd bowls, were suspended from ceiling poles. The bowls were used to serve sacred drinks during religious ceremonies and special rites. Other varied-sized clay and gourd bowls were lying haphazardly about the west side of the god house floor.

The altar was located in the center of the god house. It consisted of an eight-foot length of split mahogany plank lying directly on the ground. Nine clay pots rested side by side on the crude plank. The pots were wide-mouthed, oval, pot-bellied, and about ten inches in height. On one side, and near the top of each pot was an integrally molded figure of a god head.

The humanlike heads on the god pots were identically formed. Each had outthrust lower jaws, wide-open mouths, and exceedingly long, tapered necks. A side view of the grotesque, gaping god heads gave the impression of a row of roosters crowing simultaneously. Throat passages led to the pot interiors in order that the gods could be given food and drink during certain ceremonies and fiestas.

141

Each pot represented a particular major Maya god, who was identified by peculiarly traced designs on the heads. The patterns were so nearly alike that, except for Hachak'yum, the chief god, Jon and I never learned to identify the others. Hachak'yum was recognizable to us only because he occupied the center position on the altar board. When Jon and I had been given permission to enter the god house at will, only one restriction had been imposed. We must never, under any circumstance, step beyond an imaginary boundary line into the immediate vicinity of the altar and god pots.

The god pots are always used when a Lacandon man communes with his gods. He may worship directly in front of the altar, or he may elect to remove one or more of the sacred pots to another part of the god house. Prior to beginning his ritual he sits on one of the low stools in front of the selected pot, or pots, depending upon which of the gods are involved. The man pinches several bits from a puttylike blob of *pom*. (Pom is an incense prepared from the resin of the sacred copal tree.) The pieces of pom are deftly rolled between the fingers into small pellets, which are placed in the bottom of the god pot and ignited with a flaming strip of pitch.

When the pom is burning steadily and sending oily black smoke billowing toward the ceiling, the Lacandon begins to chant. From beginning to end, the chanter's whole being is dedicated to ritual. He is oblivious to everything and everybody around him. When the pom burns down and needs replenishing, more pellets are fed to the pot with the means of a wooden spatula. This is accomplished by the chanter without a break in the cadence or the fervor of the chant.

Most of the worshippers sat unmoving on their stools and chanted in a low monotone. Others, such as Mateo, swayed back and forth from the waist, nodded their heads to and fro, kept their eyes closed, and frequently changed the pitch of their voices. These fellows imparted an eerie, almost supernatural effect to the rituals that was spine tingling and uncomfortable to behold. Especially at night.

Never a day passed without a Lacandon entering the god house to communicate with the all-powerful deities through the medium of the pom burning pots. We photographed and sound taped some of the individual acts of worship and supplication. Mateo rendered a most impressive performance when one of his daughters became critically ill. The distraught Mateo first came to me for medical assistance; then he went to the god house. For seventy-two hours he chanted unceasingly in front of two god pots. We could easily hear his loud wailing from our hut.

143

With the passing of the hours, Mateo's voice began to weaken. It gradually diminished until on the third day, we could no longer hear him. Jon and I went to the god house to investigate. Mateo was there, swaying before the god pots. He was still chanting, but his voice was reduced to a whispering croak. We returned to the god house late that night. Mateo was hunched over the smoking pots. His face was covered with a film of grimy oil deposited by the enveloping smoke of the burning incense. Mateo's lips were moving, but there was no audible voice, only the tortured rasping of an exhausted man.

On the morning of the fourth day Mateo's daughter showed a marked improvement in her condition. Mateo staggered home from the god house. The poor man was unable to speak for a full week. In a large measure, credit for the stricken girl's recovery must be given to the medicines I had administered to her. But I cannot honestly discount the intangible benefits of Mateo's deep and abiding faith in the power and mercy of his pagan gods.

A large conch shell was suspended by a woven length of bark from a corner pole of the god house. I was curious as to where the Lacandons had obtained the shell, as Na'ha village is a considerable and difficult distance from the Gulf of Mexico, the Caribbean Sea, or the Pacific Ocean.

No one could tell me where the conch shell had come from. The men only knew that it had been at the god house for as long as they could remember.

As a young man, Chan K'in had followed the ancient practice of blowing on the conch shell from the four corners of the god house as a means of calling the gods to the god house to participate in fiestas and ceremonies. After blowing the shell on one such occasion, Chan K'in dreamed that he heard the sound of the conch again. The following day his number one wife died from the bite of a venomous snake. After this tragedy, Chan K'in blew the conch shell to summon the gods. That night he saw the shell in a dream. Within a few hours after the dream, one of his children was bitten by the fer-de-lance and died. Chan K'in declared the conch shell to be an instrument of Ky'sin, the god of the underworld. The conch has not been blown since.

The area in front of the god house was cleared of brush and trees. In the center of the clearing a ten-foot-long dugout canoe rested upside-down on crossed pole uprights. The dugout was covered with several layers of dried corn husks. The canoe had not been constructed for use on water. Its sole purpose was for the preparation and containment of sacred beverages.

Because the gods have decreed that women

145

are unclean, they are not permitted to enter the god house, nor to participate in sacred ceremonies conducted therein. The making of god pots, bowls, or any item that would be used in the god house is also reserved for the men only. The god house is more than a sacred sanctuary for the men. It also serves as a sort of stag club. In the manner of their civilized counterparts, harrassed Lacandon husbands cherish the god house as a hideout where they can temporarily remove themselves from gibbering wives and noisy, swarming children.

After a solar or lunar eclipse, the god house and everything in it but the god pots, is burned to the ground. The god pots are carried from the village by one man, and hidden in a sacred cave. Only he will ever know the location of the retired pots. When the god house and its contents have been completely burned, a new house will be erected at a site well away from the location of the old one. The men and the older boys will busy themselves in the crafting of religious objects and furnishings for the new god house. A new altar board will be graced with nine newly created god pots.

Shortly after the January occurrence of the total eclipse of the moon, the Lacandons began talking about burning the god house, and commencing the building of a new one. Chan K'in

146

said that nothing concrete would be done in the matter until after the April planting time.

Each year, before the April corn planting, the Lacandons conduct an important ceremony called the *Sa*. Chan K'in, Jr. explained that the purpose of the ceremony is to feed the major gods samples of the various fruits and vegetables both native and cultivated, used in the Lacandon diet. At the same time, the gods are asked to be benevolent during the planting of the corn, that the new crops will flourish, and that the next harvest will be generous. From personal observation of the conduct of the ceremony, it appeared that the proceedings were a form of thanksgiving that was given before the planting of the corn, rather than after the harvest.

Preparations for the Sa began at dawn. Three women gathered at the sacred kitchen and ground a huge quantity of corn into a fine meal. The corn was ground in a hand-cranked grinder that had been manufactured in Mexico City. In addition to the grinder at the sacred kitchen, Chan K'in's wives owned one, and there was another used by Mateo's two wives. In the event of the corn grinders' breaking down, there was a traditional stone metate that could be used to crush the corn into meal.

The women who were not involved in the

corn grinding busied themselves in preparing samples of the available foods native to the Lacandon diet. These portions included tortillas, beans, squash, chayote, and other foods. Meat dishes were not included in the selection.

Two men went to the god house and filled the sacred canoe with chopped pieces of sugar cane stalks. The juice of the sugar cane was extracted by pounding the stalks into a pulp, using the butt-ends of long poles. When the extraction was completed, the pulp was removed from the dugout and discarded. The sugar cane juice filled nearly half of the canoe, and was left to ferment until the following day.

In the god house, a man prepared a supply of pom pellets. The pellets were individually placed in tight rows on a large, hewn square of mahogany. On the day of the Sa celebration, the pellets of copal pitch would burn as incense in each of the nine god pots on the altar.

At sunrise the next morning, a woman entered the sacred kitchen and kindled two wood fires. Two clay pots, each with a capacity of eight gallons, were brought to the kitchen. The mound of corn meal which had been ground the previous day was divided equally between the two pots. Two men carried the sugar cane juice from the sacred canoe in large gourds and poured it in equal amounts into the pots.

148

The corn meal and sugar cane juice filled the pots about one-half full. Water was added to bring the level nearly to the top of the containers. The pots were placed on the fires and mixtures allowed to cook slowly, for nearly five hours. A woman tended each pot, frequently stirring the creamy, white contents with a wooden paddle, and stoking the fires when necessary.

At ten o'clock in the morning, the god house was ready for the ceremony to begin. The ground in front of the altar was covered with overlapping, fresh banana leaves. A number of gourd bowls were clustered on the leaves. Each bowl contained a portion of the food samples prepared by the women on the previous day. A man entered the god house and placed the pom pellets in the god pots and lighted them. When the pom was burning well, and the black smoke began curling from the god pots to the blackened roof of the god house, the man seated himself on the banana leaves, facing the altar.

The observance of Sa officially began when the Lacandon sitting in front of the altar began feeding the gods. He accomplished this by dipping a wooden spoon into a gourd bowl of prepared food, and depositing the morsel into the open throat of a god head. The food offering was semiliquid and flowed readily down the elevated neck of the god head, into the bottom of

149

the pot, where it was consumed by the burning pom. The procedure continued until each of the nine gods had received his share of the food, and a portion of the corn and sugar cane mixture from the sacred kitchen. During the feeding of the gods, the man conducting the rites chanted in a low monotone.

When the gods had been fed, all of the men gathered at the front of the god house and sat on the ground. A young man carried empty gourd bowls to the sacred kitchen, where the women filled them with the cooked Sa mixture, now thick, white, and semiliquid. The man carried the filled bowls, one at a time, back to the waiting men at the god house. When all of the men had been served a bowl, Chan K'in spooned a mouthful of Sa, and the others followed suit.

Chan K'in, and two other men used a wooden spoon. The rest drank the Sa directly from the gourd bowls. Estelle, Jon, and I were each given a bowlful of the stuff. It had a lingering, bittersweet flavor. We felt honored to have been included as members in the solemn ceremony.

As soon as a man's bowl was emptied, the young man who had filled it originally dashed to the sacred kitchen for a refill. The men consumed about ten gallons of Sa before deciding that they had enough. Only then did the women and children, who had been patiently waiting at the

150

sacred kitchen, hurriedly devour the remaining Sa. When it was all over, the men loafed at the god house for the rest of the day, talking, sleeping, and smoking cigars. The women left the sacred kitchen as soon as they had finished consuming the Sa, and went about their regular work.

During the course of one frequently observed religious ceremony, all of the Lacandon men and women have spots daubed on their faces and clothing. A red dye, derived from the berry of the achote tree, and representing blood, is used for the spotting. The men receive a spot on their foreheads and the women on their chins. The upper clothing of both sexes is liberally spotted without regard to pattern or design. Neither Chan K'in, Jr., nor his father, could clearly explain the true meaning or intent of the applied spots.

It was clear that the Lacandons have observed the spotting ceremony since the days when the Maya gods were living at Palenque. It all began when Hachak'yum learned that a group of evil men were plotting to kill him, and also destroy the world. Hachak'yum countered by summoning the men involved in the plot to his pyramid to participate in a special religious observance. The nature of the ceremony was so important that the men could not refuse to attend.

151

When all of the men had gathered at his pyramid, Hachak'yum had them seized and held prisoner. Their heads were cut off and the blood was captured in a huge pot. The headless corpses were tossed into a pit where they were devoured by sacred jaguars.

The juice of the red achote berries was blended with the blood of the slain men. The mixture was used to paint pictures on the walls of the major gods' homes. Some of the most important of the minor gods also had pictures painted upon the walls of their homes. (This account may explain the origin of the famous painted murals discovered at Bonampak.)

We found the Lacandon people extremely honest and trustworthy. They did not safeguard items that were considered valuable, except for the .22 caliber rifle ammunition I rationed the men each week. The ammunition was never displayed or talked about, but kept secreted in a place known only to the owner. The basic nature of the Lacandons precludes their forgiving, or forgetting personal affronts and injustices. They seldom quarrel, but when arguments do erupt, the consequences can be disastrous.

Chan K'in told us that shortly after his episode of terror with the federal soldiers, his wife was bitten by a fer-de-lance and died. He subsequently purchased his present number one wife, Chan Nuk, who had been widowed as the result of a fierce quarrel, in which her husband macheted her father to death. Her brother then slew him in revenge.

Several years ago one of Chan K'in's eldest daughters was shot through the face by an assailant. She was on the verge of death when the Lacandons somehow relayed word of the girl's condition to Trudy Blom. Trudy arranged to have the girl flown to a hospital in Mexico City. She recovered, but was left with a badly disfigured face. The man accused of the shooting took himself and family into exile. Some months later the true assailant's identity was discovered. He placed himself in permanent exile from Na'ha village. The innocent man and his family returned to their home in the village.

The girl who had been shot eventually married. Her husband died from snakebite. She married again. The second husband found her unsuitable, and paid Chan K'in 1,000 pesos to take her back. We came to know the unfortunate girl well, and considered her to be a gentle, sweet, and affectionate person. We felt a deep sympathy for her, as we did for all of the Lacandons. Tragedy is an ever-present specter at Na'ha. Sooner or later, every individual there must meet it head on.

During our stay at Na'ha village, Chan K'in

153

received a message via the rapid jungle grapevine that two men had been macheted to death at Yaxchilan by a fellow Lacandon. The three men had been fighting over possession of a woman.

Persons guilty of violating tribal laws or customs are judged and punished by the gods. Chan K'in said that if he, or any Lacandon sat in judgement of a fellow human being, it would be a usurpation of the authority of the gods. When a serious crime, such as murder, is committed, the guilty party obeys the will of the gods and exiles himself permanently from his village. He may, however, be accepted as a resident in another village. The final determination of the punishment for his crime will come after his death. The gods will then pass a final judgement. He will be allowed to enter their domain, or he will be sentenced to stay in the underworld realm of Ky'sin forever.

The primitive Lacandons have an unreasoning fear of the unknown and the mysterious. Hence, their superstitions are many and exert a profound influence upon their daily lives. Dreams nearly always convey bad omens. If a Lacandon dreams of floating in the air, a member of his immediate family will die soon. To dream of experiencing a toothache, and the pain is intense, a member of the family will perish. Should the pain of the toothache be only moderate, a close

154

relative will die. Dreaming of a red tomato indicates that a baby is slated for death. To drop and break a water jug in a dream signifies that a close family member will expire.

In addition to dreams, there are a great many other omens the Lacandons must be aware of, and in some cases, guard against. When a green snake is seen, the viewer will die, unless he cuts the reptile into nine pieces.

When a particular species of owl, called *buh* hoots near the village in the early hours of the night, the Lacandons are being warned that they will have visitors on the next day. The visitors will be native, that is, Lacandons from another village, or perhaps some Tzeltal Indians passing through on the trail. We heard the warning hoots of the buh on five different occasions. Each morning, following the buh's prophetic cry, traveling Tzeltals came through the village.

The dismal yowl of the *hyok,* a large nocturnal cat with spotted fur, and ears and tail like a monkey, signals the coming of visitors from the outside world. On four widely separate nights we heard the hyok's lonely squall in the nearby jungle. Following three of the warnings, Trudy Blom brought visitors to Na'ha, flown in by Pepe Martinez. The day after the fourth warning, a Wycliff Language Institute plane from Yashoquintela landed with two passengers, John and

155

Kathie Watters. The young married couple were students at the Jungle Survival School of Yashoquintela, and would spend eight weeks in a shelter north of Lake Na'ha, putting to the test the survival techniques they had learned in the classroom. A supervisor would visit them periodically to rate their progress, and after a successful solution to the survival test, they would be ready to go on toward their ultimate assignment in Africa. We were happy to have John and Kathie as our jungle neighbors, and we became good friends.

The Lacandons are justifiably afraid of the mighty jaguar. Normally a night prowler, the beautiful jungle lord is seldom seen. A jaguar prowled the village on a dark night for an interminable period. His deep-throated rumblings caused the children to cry, the dogs to bark, and the women to stoke the hut fires high and bright. We stifled our shivering curiosity deep in the lower recesses of our sleeping bags. After the jaguar betook himself to the jungle, our slumber was slow in returning. The nearness of the awesome big cat left a lasting impression.

Near ten o'clock one Sunday morning, a jaguar strolled casually through the south end of the village. All outside activities ceased as the men, women, and children, followed by the whimpering dogs, fled to the safety of their huts.

The brash young man we called Puck came running out of his hut with a .22 caliber rifle and fired one shot in the general direction of the jaguar. I was thankful that the shot went wild. Had he wounded the powerful and swift beast, the result could have been an instant disaster for the brave, but foolish Puck.

A few moments after the jaguar incident, a strange event took place. A small brown deer ran through the village, following the exact route the jaguar had taken, almost as though it was chasing the cat. This time, the reaction of the Lacandons was different. Three men hurriedly located their rifles and chased the deer into the jungle, apparently oblivious to the fact that the jaguar could not be far ahead. They returned to the village about an hour later, almost out of breath. The deer had eluded them, and they had not seen the jaguar again.

On the extremely rare occasion when a Lacandon must travel through the jungles at night, he believes that his only sure protection against a possible jaguar attack is the constant singing of a centuries old Maya song, especially composed to lull any lurking jaguars to sleep. Old Chan K'in sang the song for us one dark night. He sang softly, and although we could not understand the words, the old man's tonal quality gave his rendition an eerie, almost hypnotic effect. Jon

157

recorded the singing on tape. He played it back, and Chan K'in was so delighted with what he heard, he requested Jon to replay the tape several times.

The thing most feared by the Lacandons is a creature they call the *kisni'aka,* which lives on the blood of human beings. The kisni'aka is never seen during daylight hours. It becomes an animal at dawn and sleeps all day in a hidden rock cave. In the dark of night, when there is no moon shining, the kisni'aka reverts to a giant, hairy man-beast with a horrible face, bright green lips, and very sharp, protruding, tusklike blue teeth. It walks upright like a man and roams the jungles at night searching for unwary Lacandon men, women, and children, to kill and satisfy its insatiable thirst for warm blood.

The kisni'aka overpowers his victims by brute strength. He kills them by crouching on their chests, and sucking their breaths. When the victims are lifeless, the monster pierces their throats with its blue fangs and drinks their blood.

Chan K'in recounted a time when he and a companion were walking to Ocosingo. One night, as they slept beside the trail, the campfire burned out. Chan K'in was awakened by loud noises, and saw that his companion was being attacked by a kisni'aka. Chan K'in picked up his machete, and waving it in the air, he ran yelling and screaming

158

toward the kisni'aka. When the startled monster turned toward him, his intended victim fled into the night. Chan K'in threw the machete into the oncoming creature's face, and ran. Later, when the monster had disappeared, the two men returned to their camp. They built a large fire and sat awake and alert for the remainder of the night. The kisni'aka did not return.

One moonless night we were startled awake by the yelping of dogs. The huts were immediately a bedlam of excited and frightened voices, punctuated by scattered rifleshots. We peered through the openings in the pole walls of our hut, but could see nothing. It was almost an hour before the uproar died down and the village was once again quiet.

The next morning we were informed that a kisni'aka had prowled the village during the previous night, and that it had tried to enter several of the dwellings. In dead seriousness, Chan K'in informed us that it was extremely dangerous for us to go to sleep at night without a fire burning in our hut. Fire was the best protection against the attack of the blood-thirsty, blue-toothed monster. We did not follow the old fellow's advice. Nevertheless, each time thereafter when we were awakened by strange sounds in the night, our first thoughts were of the kisni'aka.

159

We were frequently awakened by events and noises that had galvanized the Lacandons into action. At three o'clock one morning, Jon and I, and half of the villagers were brought bolt upright by Estelle's sudden screaming and crying. She had been aroused by the thumping and lurching of a small worm that had crawled into her ear and become entrapped. I collected my wits sufficiently to get a cup of water and a spoon, and flush the little worm out of her ear. The next morning, of course, we had to explain to the curious Lacandons what had happened. I admired their calm acceptance of the story. Puck, and one other young man, were the only ones who showed amusement.

burning. While waiting for the vegetation to dry, the men's daily routine took on a more leisurely pace. Other than hunting game, they were free to loaf about their huts or in the god house.

The women's responsibilities did not slacken, however. They continued working at their myriad tasks from dawn to dusk. The young girls helped the women. Except for the onerous chores of gathering firewood and toting water, the seven- to twelve-year-old boys had nothing to do but play and entertain themselves. I had noticed that each afternoon Ky'um, and several other young lads, left the village and remained absent for a considerable length of time. One afternoon I stopped the boys and asked them where they were going, and what they planned to do when they arrived. Ky'um insisted that I come with them and learn for myself. I hung a movie camera over one shoulder, a still camera over the other, and tagged after the group.

About a half-mile from the village we arrived at a thickly forested area containing tall and closely spaced mahogany and sapadillo trees. The lowest branches of the trees were at least fifty feet above the ground. Hanging from every limb were liana vines of two-inch diameter that reached to the jungle floor. The deep shadow of the area was broken by narrow lances of sunlight that speared through the high umbrella of dense, leafy

162

branches. This was the boys' natural playground. It was pure exhilaration to watch and film the little fellows and their monkeylike antics as they swung on the vines from one huge tree to another, yelling like miniature Tarzans.

Most of the clothing worn by the Lacandons is fashioned from bolt cloth, procured in San Cristobal and Tenosique. Needles and thread are also obtained from the outside. The older women scorn the manufactured cloth, and weave a coarse homespun from native cotton to make the poncholike gowns worn by their husbands.

The spinning and weaving techniques are the same as those employed by the Maya women of a thousand years ago. In the spinning process, the raw cotton is held in the left hand, or sometimes thrown over the left shoulder. The cotton is converted into thread by means of a mahogany spindle, which consists of a slender, pointed stick about ten inches in length, and weighted at the pointed end with a disk of baked clay. The disk gives weight and balance to the spindle as it is twirled between the thumb and forefinger of the right hand. In use, the pointed end of the spindle rests in a small plate made of clay. When the fast turning spindle becomes filled the woman transfers the coarse, heavy thread to a loosely wound ball.

After a sufficient supply of thread has been spun, the woman turns her attention to the weaving of the cloth. This is accomplished on a crude backstrap loom. A mahogany rod is attached at each end of the warp to keep the woven cloth stretched to the desired width. The upper end of the loom is tied about four feet above the ground to an upright pole. A wide band of cotton cloth is tied to the ends of the lower loom rod, forming a large loop. This loop passes behind the weaver, resting just above the hipline. When the weaver, who sits on the ground while working, wants to tighten the warp, she leans backward against the back loop. When slack is desired in order to introduce new lines of thread, the weaver leans forward. The finished material is a closely woven, heavy piece of cloth about two and one-half feet wide, and seven feet in length.

One day, Chan Nuk, the number one wife of Chan K'in, set up her loom and began weaving. The old woman worked but a short time each day, and then only when the sun was shining. I followed the weaving process closely, photographing the various stages of progress. The old woman ignored my regular presence and concentrated her total attention on the weaving. I made note of the number of hours Chan Nuk devoted to weaving the cloth. The total was approximately fifty hours. It required but a short time for Chan Nuk to fold the length of homespun and convert it to a gown by sewing the two sides and the top, leaving openings for the head and arms of the prospective wearer, whom I had supposed would be Chan K'in.

I was speechless, and of course, overjoyed when Chan K'in presented the completed garment to me as a gift from him and Chan Nuk. The great interest I had consistently shown while his wife wove and assembled the garment had made both of them feel that I wanted it. I was their friend, and they gave it to me. It was so touchingly and beautifully simple. And, as with all of the many gifts bestowed upon us by the kind and generous Lacandons, there was nothing expected in return.

I tried the gown on one late afternoon. It fit tightly across my shoulders, and the hem was higher above my knees than the Lacandons wear the gowns. Estelle and Jon suggested that perhaps the Lacandon people would enjoy a style show. I deviated from custom and wore a pair of shorts beneath the gown. I also donned a pair of low-quarter tennis shoes, without socks. Estelle and Jon armed themselves with cameras, and the three of us stepped out of our hut to begin an unannounced tour of the village.

The people's reaction was instantaneous and hilarious. Men, women, and children ran out of

165

their huts to stand and stare in open-mouthed wonder, which changed immediately to hysterical, whooping laughter. Some of the young men fell to the ground, doubled over in uncontrolled mirth. For the first time since coming to Na'ha, we saw the leathery, wrinkled face of Chan Nuk break into a smile.

We stopped in front of Chan K'in's hut where we were joined by the entire village population, who continued pointing at me, laughing, and talking loudly to each other. It was indeed a carnival atmosphere and we enjoyed it immensely. Each of Chan K'in's three wives posed with me for pictures. The youngest was carrying her few-weeks-old baby. I held the infant in my arms, and the young mother stood by my side while Jon shuttered the camera.

It was only fitting and proper that I pose with the one who had made my new gown. I stood beside old Chan Nuk, with an arm about her labor-bent shoulders. The old woman was chewing on a smouldering cigar. She said something to her husband, who responded by lighting a cigar and giving it to me. Jon was ready to take the picture, but we were interrupted again. Chan K'in, grinning happily, thrust his machete in my hand. Now I was indeed a Lacandon, for I had a woman, a fine new gown, a cigar, and a machete!

166

With my bright blue eyes, deeply sun-bronzed face, neck, and arms, and my legs almost a lily white, I presented a ludicrous sight to the Lacandons. They, and we, had a genuinely happy experience together, and the uninhibited amusement enjoyed by all bound the growing ties of understanding and friendship ever tighter.

The jungle environment was full of startling, sometimes dangerous surprises. I awakened one morning to find tiny blood blisters, and an angry red rash covering the back of my left hand. The itching was constant and almost unbearable. Somewhere in the village area, or perhaps along the trail to the lake shore, I had unwittingly come in contact with a leaf of the poisonous chechem negra tree. The Lacandons informed me that if the condition was not immediately checked, the violent rash and blood blisters would spread generally over my body and leave me incapacitated. They wanted to apply a mixture of wood ash, lemon juice, and salt to the afflicted area.

I appreciated their concern, but I declined their remedy. I applied a generous coating of medicated ointment to the poisoned area of my hand, and covered it loosely with a sterile gauze dressing and bandage. If my medicine did not clear up the chechem negra problem, I would try the Lacandons' method. After several miserable days and nights the intense itching stopped,

167

and the blood blisters dried. Within ten days, my hand was completely healed.

One night the village was assaulted by gale winds and a downpour of rain. Estelle and I had early sought the comfort of our sleeping bags. Jon was sitting on the floor, writing in his journal by the light of the fire. A fiercely droning insect, almost an inch in length, flew into the hut. It landed on Jon's leg and immediately attempted to bite through his heavy denim trousers. Jon hurriedly brushed the beetlelike invader from his leg. It flew back and again tried to bite him. Jon struck the insect and the hard blow stunned it. He wanted to kill the persistent attacker, but he did not want to crush it, for it was so unusual in size and appearance that he wanted to examine the insect by the light of day. Jon wrapped the insect in a bit of foil and placed it on the hot coals of the fire for a few minutes until he thought it was dead.

The following morning I spread a white cloth over a large flat rock in front of our hut. Jon carefully removed the lifeless insect from the foil wrapper and placed it on the cloth. The insect had a mottled coloring of dark green, gray, and deep brown. Its transparent membrane wings had a spread of about two inches. The mandible was large, and a quarter-inch long proboscis curved backward like the tusks of a boar. The heavy body was shaped like a shield, with two small, curved, mastlike members at the extreme rear end. The insect had four legs, each decorated with horizontal dark and light bands. The under side of the body was the color of a turtle's lower shell, and it was shaped like a hydroplane.

We were busy photographing and sketching the insect when two Lacandon men stopped to see what we were doing. When they saw the insect they quickly stepped backward, obviously frightened. With great excitement they explained that the beetle we were so nonchalantly handling was a *mokochi'ha*, extremely dangerous, and the bite of which was almost as perilous as that of the nahayuka, or fer-de-lance snake. The men said that the mokochi'ha was nocturnal in nature, and that it was normally found near lakes or other large bodies of water. It seemed that Jon had encountered only a baby, for the mokochi'ha reportedly grows to a mature length of nearly five inches.

There was a chilling finale to the mokochi'ha incident. After completing our examination of the mokochi'ha, we left it lying on the cloth while we carried the cameras and sketching materials into the hut. When we came back outside we were astonished to see the mokochi'ha flex its wings several times, and then soar into the

169

air, droning its way toward the lake. We had been confidently and carelessly handling a live killer.

When we first came to Chiapas, we had been warned of a large, blue-winged fly that is native to the Selva Lacandon, and is considered to be dangerous. Called the *mosca chiclera,* its bite causes sloughing ulcerations of the skin that are very difficult to heal. Although we did not see a mosca chiclera while we were at Na'ha, the Lacondons verified its existence.

One of the young men named Chan Bor discovered a cave while hunting in the mountains south of Lake Na'ha. When Jon and I expressed a keen interest in exploring his find, Chan Bor volunteered to lead us to the cave. Jon and I put a length of rope, a flashlight, camera gear, candles, extra matches, and a first aid kit in a pack. Chan Bor, accompanied by Ky'um, led us away from the village by a trail that wound into the mountains.

The mountains were steep and heavily forested, with an almost impassable undergrowth of vines, ferns, thorny bushes, and windfallen tree trunks. About three miles from the village the boys left the trail. They easily made their way through the undergrowth, pausing frequently to allow Jon and me to catch up.

We stopped for a rest beneath the branches

of a huge sapadillo tree. Chan Bor picked up a pear-shaped object that had fallen from the upper reaches of the tree. He stripped away the thin brown husk that covered what Chan Bor said was the fruit of the sapadillo, or gum tree. He indicated that Jon and I should eat the fruit. We found it delicious. Chan Bor and Ky'um searched around the base of the tree and found more of the fruit. They gave us one more, and ate several themselves. Ky'um said that the fruit of the sapadillo was a favored delicacy among his people.

Chan Bor slashed the trunk of the tree with his machete. Almost immediately the deep gash began to weep a milky sap, which is the base for the civilized world's chewing gum. We tasted the bittersweet sap and did not like it.

We arrived at the cave site after a two-mile walk from the trail. It was located on the slope of a mountain ridge, with its entrance almost hidden beneath thick foliage. As Jon and I made preparations to enter the cave, our companions began to exhibit an increasing nervousness and excitement. When we entered the cave opening, Ky'um came with us. Chan Bor said that he would wait for us outside.

The three of us advanced slowly and carefully along the rocky floor of the cave, which led slightly downward. The low ceiling caused us to walk in a low crouch. The floor was littered with gnawed and splintered pieces of bones. About ten feet inside the passageway there was a large depression in the cave floor, near a wall. Ky'um examined several tufts of animal hair or fur, and said that a *ba'room* (jaguar) had slept or reposed there many times. He also related the chilling news that if a ba'room was in the cave, he undoubtedly had heard our approach and entrance, and would be crouched and waiting somewhere in the deeper recesses of the cave. I shined my flashlight down the corridor. The bright light revealed that the cave made an abrupt right angle turn about thirty feet ahead of us. Jon wanted to proceed, at least to the cave's turning point. I was not eager to pursue the exploration further. Ky'um warned that if a jaguar should be in the cave, it would charge us without so much as a warning growl.

A large vampire bat, suspended from the ceiling, drew our attention. Jon and I moved a few feet forward to better observe the bat, and to get into position for a close-up photograph of the extremely nauseous-looking mammal. I wasted too much time preparing for the shot, and the vampire flew deeper into the cave. An ominous-looking black spider about five inches in diameter likewise escaped the camera lens by scuttling into a nearby crevice in the cave wall.

172

The obviously frightened Ky'um held his ground while Jon and I slowly made our way toward the bend in the cave. When we reached the turn Jon shone his light forward into a vast room containing dead stalagmites and stalactites. The ceiling was black with suspended vampire bats. We did not advance beyond the bend in the cave, for the vampires became disturbed, and some began to fly past us. When they reached the bright light at the cave's entrance, they reversed their flight and swished uncomfortably close to our ears on their return to the interior. Ky'um cautioned us that if sufficiently provoked, the vampires would attack, and that the bites inflicted by them would cause the blood to flow, thereby encouraging more onslaughts. He also told us that the bite of the vampire was poisonous.

I did not relish the prospect of a possible encounter with an enraged jaguar, and I have a deep-rooted aversion to bats, particularly when their wing tips are literally brushing my cheeks. Accordingly, our cave exploration came to an end, and we scrambled over the boulder-strewn floor to the exit, and the waiting Chan Bor.

Ky'um was very happy and relieved to be out of the strange cave. He asked me for a cigarette, something he had not done before. I was thoroughly impressed with the boy's Spartan-like be-

173

havior during our stay in the cave. All of his native instincts, superstitions, and fears had strongly urged him to flee the darkness of the unknown cave, and escape to the safety of the known world of daylight. Yet, the little fellow had resolutely remained with us. Of such stuff is true bravery composed.

Preceded by Chan Bor and Ky'um, we left the cave site and started walking back through the forest to the trail. Jon and I were plodding along slowly, fighting the tangled vegetation. We looked ahead toward our young guides. They had disappeared. We called out the boys' names, but there was no response. We stood in place for several minutes, looking, listening, and frequently shouting for Chan Bor and Ky'um, but to no avail.

Jon suggested that the boys might have decided to desert us, and were now well on their way back to the village. He worried that on our own, we might become lost in the jungled mountains. On our way to the cave I had paid scant attention to possible landmarks for the return trip, confident that our guides would lead us back to the trail. Now I was not so sure that I could find the trail again, although I assured my son that I could.

We had just passed two huge, closely spaced mahogany trees when the silence of the forest was

174

shattered by the roar of a jaguar. The blood-freezing sound came from directly behind us. We raised our machetes in an instinctive, but ridiculous, defense and turned swiftly about to face the charge. There was no leaping jaguar. Chan Bor and Ky'um stood beside the trees, where they had hidden and awaited us with the hair-raising ambush. The shock of the experience left Jon and me numb. It prompted our two mischievous imps into a frenzy of riotous laughter that caused tears to roll down their cheeks. Jon and I swallowed our choking lumps of terror and congratulated the boys on their clever coup.

During the remainder of the route back to the trail, and on to the village, we played hide-and-seek, and jaguar games with our fun-loving guides. They were happy that we would join with them in their boyish pranks and capers, and they made the most of it. They also made the day one of our most memorable at Na'ha.

There were several small transistor radios in possession of the Lacandons. Like Jorge's golden wristwatch, the radios had probably been given to the Indians by visitors from the outside. Only one radio, owned by Chan K'in, Jr., was operational. He rarely turned it on, and then only to listen to music for a short period of time. The other sets in the village were silenced until the acquisition of hard-to-get replacement batteries.

The men must have occasionally listened to news from the outside world, for they were aware of the fact that men had walked on the surface of the moon. I probed old Chan K'in's feelings about this tremendous achievement. He was not favorably impressed, muttering that man's consorting with Ak'na would only result in bringing more evil into men's hearts, giving them yet another senseless reason to kill one another.

That the Lacandons enjoy music was evidenced by their listening to it via radio. However, other than a limited number of traditional and chanted ballads, such as the one designed to keep the jaguar at bay when a Lacandon is on the trail at night, the people of Na'ha have no music that is native to their culture. They do have a flute, a drum, and a gourd rattle, all patterned after like instruments of old. Sadly, no one knew how to play them. Only Chan K'in, Chan K'in, Jr., and young Ky'um knew how to construct the instruments. The very few flutes, drums, and gourd rattles made are for transport and sale in the market at Tenosique.

We were privileged to observe the step by step construction of a drum by old Chan K'in. The body of the drum consisted of a clay jar with an oval mouth about six inches in diameter. With a god head (the god of music) molded on the side of the jar, it looked like a sacred god pot, except that the lower section was larger and more balloonlike and the entire jar was about five inches taller.

While Chan K'in was molding and firing the clay jar, one of his wives prepared the drum head. This consisted of a piece of deerskin that had been scraped clean of hair and sinew months before, and had been stored against the day of its use. The wife spent hours working the stiff deerskin with her fingers until it became soft and pliable. There must have been some method of treating the skin originally to prevent decomposition, but I was not able to learn how this might have been accomplished.

The third phase of construction involved fastening the deerskin head over the mouth of the drum jar. Chan K'in went into the jungle and returned with a long green vine that was about one-half inch in diameter. Using a small knife, the old man carefully shaved three long and very thin strips from the vine stem. During this operation I noticed that the knife Chan K'in was using was quite dull. I procured a whet stone from my gear and honed the blade to a razor sharpness. When the old man resumed slicing the vine strips, the blade slid easily through the soft fiber. The sharp blade also shaved about half of the time the dull one would have required to cut the strips.

Chan K'in rewarded me with a broad smile, and a cigar.

Chan K'in braided the three long, thin strips into a circular wreath that was slightly larger than the circumference of the jar opening. He placed the piece of deerskin over the jar opening, and followed this by slipping the circle of vines over the skin and the edge of the jar top. It was a tight fit. As time went by, the drying of the vine collar would cause it to shrink, until eventually the drum head would be stretched tightly and securely bound to the top of the jar.

Chan K'in next braided two heavy vines into a circle which was less in circumference than the bottom of the drum jar. The jar was placed upon the vine circle and secured thereto by strips of bark which extended from the vine circle at the bottom, to the vine circle affixed to the top of the jar.

Drum sticks are not used in beating the drum. Sound is produced by drumming the head with the fingers of both hands. We were fortunate in being able to obtain a Lacandon drum and adding it to our prized collection of primitive Indian artifacts.

The flute is very simply made from a hollowed out wand of wood that is tipped with a carved mouthpiece.

In the making of a gourd rattle, a hole is cut

178

in the top and bottom of a specially selected gourd. The gourd is converted into a sound box by the burning of a number of tiny, evenly spaced holes around the middle of the shell. A design composed of connecting straight lines is etched with a knife around the surface of the gourd. The entire gourd is then hand rubbed to a smooth, highly polished finish. About twelve pea-sized, smooth and round pebbles are put into the gourd. A round, tapered wood handle is inserted through the holes in the top and bottom of the gourd and pushed until tightly fitted. The protruding portion of the handle at the bottom of the gourd is cut off, and the gourd rattle is completed.

I always take a harmonica with me into wilderness areas. I find that playing the instrument relaxes me, and also, it is interesting to observe the reactions of primitive peoples to the music I am able to provide. I brought two harmonicas to Na'ha. Almost every evening I sat on a rock in front of our hut and played. At the first notes, the village children would gather in front of me, and quietly listen to the serenade. At the conclusion of my music, the little ones would return to their homes.

As darkness closed over the village the older boys and the young men would congregate inside our hut for their nightly visit. The request would soon come for me to play some *musica*.

179

After several weeks of listening to renditions of the selections I like best, the fellows began to request their favorite tunes, chief among these being the music of the song "Blowing in the Wind."

One of my most intrigued listeners was a young man named K'in Bor. He was absolutely fascinated by the harmonica. At our nightly sessions he was always the first to ask that I play the instrument. If members of the fireside group began talking while I was playing a number, he asked them to be quiet. The young man could scarcely believe it when I gave him one of my harmonicas as a gift. Thereafter, late at night we would hear discordant harmonica notes coming from K'in Bor's hut.

Little Ky'um also wanted a harmonica. Too shy to ask me for it, he prevailed upon Jon to make the request for him. I told Ky'um that I would give him the harmonica the night before we left Na'ha. He flashed his beautiful smile and said that in exchange for the instrument, he would make for me two clay god pots.

The following afternoon, Ky'um began preparing the clay for the molding of the god pots. Four days later he came to me and sadly explained that his efforts had failed. The pots had not fired properly, and had disintegrated when he had tried to pick them out of the wood ashes.

He said that he would renew his efforts, and that the god pots would be finished in five days.

On the evening of the fifth day, Ky'um came to our hut with two completed god pots, one for Estelle, and one for me. They were about half the size of the sacred god pots that rested on the altar board in the god house, but they were identical in every detail except in the markings. Both pots had a base color of white. Estelle's was painted with vertical red stripes, cross-hatched with black stripes. My god pot also had the vertical red stripes, but did not have the black cross marks. The red coloring was obtained from the achote tree, the white from the ashes of burned snail shells, and the black was derived from the soot that accumulates on the underside of the hut roofs from the perpetually burning and smoking wood fires.

It was significant that Ky'um decorated Estelle's pot to represent Ak'na, the moon. Mine is symbolic of K'in, the sun. Estelle and I consider the two god pots an expression of the sincere love and adoration from an unaffected Lacandon boy.

The evening before we left Na'ha for our journey home, I gave Ky'um the harmonica. It was an appropriate gift for the sensitive Ky'um, the little "god of song."

181

The Lacandons possessed about twenty-eight chickens, which were unevenly divided into four flocks. Chan K'in's number one wife, Chan Nuk, owned eight of them. His number two woman had six hens. The remainder of the fowl were divided between the wives of Mateo, and the wife of another Chan K'in, whom we called Antonio.

The chickens were scrawny, rawboned, barenecked, and generally without their tail feathers. Originally provided in large numbers by the federal government, the chickens had been reduced in number by improper care and shelter, disease, and foraging predators. The chickens were not eaten by the Lacandons, but were maintained for the egg output, which was meagre, at best. There was but one bedraggled rooster, and it belonged to Chan Nuk. His necessity was debatable, since the people consumed the few eggs almost as soon as the hens laid them.

During the day, the chickens were free to roam the village, spending a great deal of time foraging in the huts and competing with the dogs for whatever bits of edible scraps that might be found or stolen.

At night the chickens were penned in a circular enclosure built of small upright poles, the butt ends resting on the ground to form a circle three feet in diameter. The tops of the poles met to form a conical shaped coop. A small hoop of twisted, or braided vines was dropped over the top of the poles to secure the coop. The chickens were released each morning by removing the vine hoop and taking out several of the poles from the circular wall. There were several of the coops for each flock of chickens, since one enclosure would only hold about eight chickens. The construction of the odd looking coops was extremely simple, but served to discourage night prowling predators hoping for a chicken dinner.

The women would not release the chickens from the coops until the hens had laid their eggs. This was done in order that the hens would not nest in the nearby jungle, where they would quickly fall victim to wild animals.

The chickens are occasionally fed bits of tortillas, or leftover pieces of boiled chayote, a native vegetable that grows on a vine, and tastes much like a potato. On occasion, the women went into the jungle and located a large fallen tree that was infested with termites. They chopped large chunks from the tree with machetes and carried them back to the village. The pieces were placed in an open area, where the chickens soon congregated to peck and scratch at the rotten wood, feasting upon the hundreds of fat termites found lodging within.

Chan Nuk kept her chickens in three coops

that were near our hut. When she released her chickens each day, she threw them bits of tortillas or chayotes. Almost every day she grabbed a hen out of the busily eating flock, tucked it firmly under her left armpit, and with her open right hand soundly spanked the squawking chicken on its rear end. It was a long time before we learned the reason for Chan Nuk's spanking of the chickens. Her neighbor's hens, which belonged to Chan K'in's number two wife, were released each day before Chan Nuk turned hers loose. When Chan Nuk fed her flock, one or two chickens from next door would come and strive with them for the scraps of food. This angered the ever watchful Chan Nuk. Shooing the raiders away was useless, but a solid thumping on their bottoms served its purpose, at least until the next day.

The fireflies of Na'ha are noteworthy. They are about three-quarters of an inch in length, and have double headlamps that emit intermittent bursts of brilliant, blue green light. In the late evening darkness, the flashing lights from millions of fireflies flitting at the edge of the surrounding jungle seemed to encircle the village with a halo of scintillating diamonds.

The children use the firefly as a form of late evening amusement. A small twig is harmlessly inserted under a membrane located on the un-

184

derside of the beetle's body. The firefly cannot wriggle off from the stick. After threading the firefly, the child twirls the stick. The intermittent flashing of the firefly's light is transformed into constantly lighted eccentric circles, much like the firework's sparklers twirled in the darkness by the youngsters of our society.

The Lacandon women utilize the firefly for practical purposes. They use the same techniques as the children, except that instead of one firefly, they place as many as eight on a slender stick. The combined light of the fireflies is bright enough to illuminate a dark corner of a hut. When the fireflies have served their purposes, whether for play, or as torches, they are removed from the stick and allowed to fly free, none the worse for their experience.

Government attempts to assist the Lacandons meet with little success. Agricultural agents have come to Na'ha. Enlisting the Lacandons' help, they have cleared garden plots and planted a variety of vegetables considered suitable for growth in the area's climatic conditions. After the garden has been planted, the agent gives carefully worded instructions to the Lacandons on the future care of the garden. His work finished, he departs for the outside world.

There was a large vegetable garden at Na'ha

185

village that had been organized by an agricultural agent a short time before our arrival. The Lacandons had neglected to follow the agent's instructions, and the one-month-old garden was matted with weeds and grass. A few heads of lettuce had managed to partly develop and could be seen through the dense cover of weeds. Within a few weeks of our arrival the garden area was almost entirely reclaimed by the jungle.

Government agents fly to Na'ha with mahogany seedlings and young coffee shrubs and plant them in abandoned milpa areas. The Lacandons are encouraged to care for the shrubs and trees until they are self-sufficient, for one day the people will reap monetary rewards from the sale of coffee beans, and lumber.

The Lacandons are not impressed with the long range promises of such programs. The help that they would readily understand and accept are medical programs, blankets, and other critical needs of the moment. A remark by Chan K'in graphically underscores the fatalistic character of the Lacandons. He said, "The mahogany trees will not mature for fifty years. It will be ten years before the coffee plants produce beans. How can these things be of use to us? Most, if not all of us will be dead by that time."

The Lacandons know, and calmly accept the fact that they are doomed to extinction. The

186

gods told their ancestors hundreds of years ago that white *nachi'surs* (foreigners) would invade their land from the east and from the north, and one day, the Lacandons would cease to exist. The gods told them, too, that when the last Lacandon dies, that will signal the end of all human life on earth.

I was busily engaged one morning in stirring a brown cane sugar and liquified powdered milk syrup over the fire. Chan K'in walked in, handed me two freshly rolled cigars, and hunched himself beside me. He watched intently as I continued to stir the slowly boiling mixture. He asked me what I was doing. I explained that I was trying to make oatmeal and sugar candy. I promised that if my efforts were successful, I would bring him some. His grunted, unintelligible reply gave me the impression that he was not in favor of a man doing a woman's work. After several minutes of stony silence, the old fellow sauntered off to his hut.

When I finished cooking the syrup, the hair was burned from the back of my hands, my eyes were red and weepy from the smoke and heat, but I had made two dozen oatmeal candy mounds that were quite tasty. Estelle and I took four of the oatmeal candies to Chan K'in, whom we found sitting in his number one wife's kitchen.

He sampled one of the candy mounds and liked it. Chan Nuk, his number one wife, came to the kitchen. Chan K'in broke off a small bit of the candy and gave it to her. She liked it, but the old man refused to give her more. His number two wife also came by for a sample. She, too, received only a very small bite. Chan K'in had eaten all but the last mound of candy when his young wife, number three, approached and spoke to him as she pointed to the remaining piece of candy. He handed it to her. She took a bite, chewed briefly, and with an impish grin popped the rest of the mound into her mouth as she ran laughingly to her hut. Chan K'in said nothing, but grinned with pride. Pretty little Chan Nuk was his favorite wife, and she could do no wrong.

Young K'in Bor's wife was not more than fourteen years of age, and very pretty. She had recently lost her first baby. As is customary, a mother sleeps with her baby. K'in Bor's wife awakened one morning to discover that her baby had died during the night. Since the infant had not been ill, it was supposed that death had been caused by accidental suffocation.

The tragic event had drastically altered the young mother's personality. She became acutely withdrawn and uncommunicative, and ceased to mingle with the village women. She kept herself isolated in her hut, emerging only for necessary tasks. The hut was near our dwelling, and we never heard quarreling or fighting between her and K'in Bor. When he was away during the day, she frequently flew into terrible rages, during which she would turn on the family dog and beat it unmercifully with a club, or the flat side of a machete.

Our three musketeers, Ky'um, Chan K'in, and Chan Bor invited Jon and me to go fishing with them. We clambered aboard a dugout one late afternoon, and the boys paddled the canoe along the south shore of the lake. They kept the raft close to the reed-covered shallows, stopping several times to peel off their gowns and slip over the side to gather snails. The boys speared a bit of snail meat to the barb of a hook. The fishing line was a length of cotton string. No pole was used. The baited hook was lowered to the lake bottom, and I saw several very small perchlike fish dart out of the nearby reeds to investigate the bait. During the course of an hour's patient effort, the boys hooked three fish that wriggled off before they could be brought aboard the dugout.

The glassy waters of the lake mirrored the multicolored sunset and the western mountains were turning a deep purple when the boys stopped fishing and headed the dugout for the village.

There were no fish to bring home, but it had been great fun.

Lake Na'ha had at one time been infested with alligators. The once flourishing market for alligator hide products eliminated all but a few very small ones that remain hidden in the thick reeds near the shores. Chan K'in, Jr. told us of a small lake that he called *Yellow-yellow,* located several hundred yards west of Lake Na'ha. He said that the lake was teeming with alligators of all sizes. There was a trail around Lake Na'ha to Yellow-yellow, but Chan K'in, Jr. said that it would be difficult to walk it. He volunteered to take us across Lake Na'ha by dugout.

It was high noon when we began our ride across the lake toward the western shore. The skies were cloudless, the waters placid, and the sun was hot. Estelle, Jon, and I sat in the bottom of the dugout. Chan K'in, Jr. stood upright in the rear of the craft. Chan Bor stood at the bow. The young men's dark mahogany faces glistened in the bright sunlight, and the flat, sinewy muscles of their arms rippled, as they skillfully wielded the long paddles. The heavy dugout sliced smoothly and swiftly through the clear azure waters, leaving a sparkling wake astern.

I asked Chan K'in, Jr. if I might paddle the dugout. He handed me his paddle without a word and exchanged places with me. Chan Bor ceased paddling at the bow and sat down. The motive power and guiding skill was left entirely up to me. My former experience in paddling a light, well-balanced canoe stood me in little stead. The dugout, which had been knifing so straight and easily through the water became an unmanageable monster. The craft swayed and spun in circles which I was unable to control. Estelle and Jon clung desperately to the sides of the canoe, afraid of a capsize. Our young friends were in hysterical laughter. I was embarrassed. I was very happy to give the paddle back to Chan K'in, Jr. He and Chan Bor quickly put the dugout on a smooth and proper course and we glided to the west bank.

The dugout was paddled and pushed with the oars as far as possible into the reeds and fallen-tree debris that obstructed the shore. Holding to dead branches for support we walked unsteadily to the precipitous shore. We followed a seldom-used and overgrown trail up the steep slope to the top of a razor-back ridge that divided Na'ha and Yellow-yellow lakes. The ridge sides were so steep that both lakes seemed to lie at our feet.

Lake Yellow-yellow lay in a crater, the banks of which plunged into the water more than a hundred feet below us, at an angle of more than sixty degrees. A blanket of gnarled, stunted trees and thorny bushes tenaciously gripped the sides of the crater. The distance across the lake appeared to be less than a thousand yards. The lake was imprisoned in the crater. There was no outlet, and no streams emptied into the lake. Since the level of Yellow-yellow's waters appeared to be even with those of Lake Na'ha, perhaps the two were connected by underground passages.

The ridge crest was very hot. Down in the crater, the deep yellow waters of the lake were murky and flat. Extending several yards out into the water from all around the shoreline was a tangled mass of fallen and rotting trees. Weather-whitened bare branches, like skeletal fingers, grasped upward toward the vault of sky as if in a mute plea for rescue.

Two alligators, each about fourteen feet in length, surfaced near the center of the lake. They remained motionless until Chan Bor threw a rock into the water. At the instant of the rock's impact and splash the two monsters immediately and swiftly glided toward the point of disturbance. The hungry rush for what might have been food alerted a dozen more large alligators that had been lurking unseen in the clutter of dead trees floating along the banks. They quickly converged at the site below us. After a brief

192

flurry of investigation they dispersed and slowly returned to their scattered haunts.

We wondered how the large number of alligators could find sufficient food to remain alive in such a barren environment, from which there was no apparent escape. With water easily available elsewhere, it is doubtful that many large animals or birds would venture into the crater and to the deadly shores of Yellow-yellow for a drink.

Grinning broadly, Chan K'in, Jr. asked if we wanted to try a descent down the steep ridge to the lakeshore. None of us cared to take the risk. The ridge top was close enough to Yellow-yellow and its murderous inhabitants.

On our return walk to the dugout Chan K'in, Jr. pointed out a vanilla plant, from which we picked a handful of the aromatic beans. Farther down the trail he showed us a small tree with narrow, pale green leaves. He cautioned us not to touch the leaves or the tree, as the sap was extremely poisonous. He said that when a Lacandon wants to take his own life, several drops of the tree's sap is placed on the tongue. Death comes in a matter of seconds. Chan K'in, Jr. had known one man who had committed suicide in this manner. However, suicide among the Lacandons is extremely rare.

When we reached the dugout, a welcome

breeze was blowing. Scattered clouds reflected their fleeciness in the lake's blue waters. The young men paddled the dugout along the south shore to a small cove that was clear of reeds. Chan Bor pushed his paddle into the soft lake bottom until only a part of the handle remained above water. He anchored the dugout to the protruding handle with a short length of vine. The young men asked if we would like to go swimming. We declined. They jumped into the lake for a cooling dip, pulled themselves back into the dugout, and we returned to the village.

Chan K'in consented to pose with his three wives and fourteen children for pictures. We had scheduled the photography for late in the afternoon, a time when no one would have to neglect their work to gather in the open area in front of Chan K'in's hut. When we arrived with our cameras, the family members were all present, except for Chan K'in and his youngest wife. I walked to the old man's hut to tell him we were ready to begin taking pictures. I found him sitting in his hammock smoking a cigar. Chan Nuk was standng beside him, slowly and carefully combing the tangles out of his long hair. The comb was of mahogany and hand carved, with smooth and evenly spaced teeth on both sides. The charming scene gave ample evidence of the girl's concern for her husband's personal appearance. She wanted the old monarch to look his best for the photography.

The Lacandon people were always pleasantly cooperative when we asked them to pose for pictures. We were fortunate in procuring pictures of all of the individuals, as well as each family group in the village.

CHAPTER 7

In many ways, the hot
days of March were
akin to the time of year
we call Indian summer.
Many of the deciduous trees had exchanged the
greens of their leaves for golds, browns, reds, and

197

yellows. The jungle was always teeming with wildlife, but the tempo increased during the weeks of March. Snakes were constantly on the move. Lizards, including the large iguanas, were seemingly everywhere. Two bright green lizards, about eight inches long, took up residence in our hut. They spent most of the daylight hours peering at us from the ceiling of palmetto fronds.

A great variety of colorful moths and butterflies flitted about the village area. We had the rare privilege of observing a gorgeous monarch butterfly at close range. I estimated that the span of the black and orange wings was in excess of eight inches. Hordes of flamingo pink and glittering red dragon flies dominated the marshy lakeshores.

The region of Lake Na'ha would be a bird watchers paradise. The numbers and species of birds in the area are almost unbelievable. Jon sat in an open space behind our hut with a pair of binoculars. He observed twenty-two different types of birds in a time span of thirty minutes. I noted a half-dozen kinds of hummingbirds during our stay at Na'ha.

Various kinds of brilliantly plumed parakeets, parrots, macaws, and toucans were commonplace. In the outlying jungle there were turkey vultures, yellow-headed vultures, and the majestic king vulture, a great bird with a multicolored head,

198

silver collared neck, black tail, and black wing tips.

The true monarch of the Selva Lacandon bird kingdom is the harpy eagle. This magnificent creature measures about three feet in body length, and stands nearly two feet in height. The underbody is white, the wings black, and it has a black collar around the neck. Two tufts of feathers stand erect on the top of the bird's head, and resemble a pair of horns. The eagle's powerful legs are nearly as large in circumference as a man's wrist. Deeply curved, long black talons serve to securely grip a captured prey while the cruelly sharp upper beak of the eagle rips the victims to shreds.

The harpy eagle's favorite food victims are small monkeys. It also preys on little children left unattended in the open. According to the Indians, the harpy has attacked and killed men and women. We saw one of the fearsome eagles. Its overall fierce appearance and baleful yellow eyes made us shudder.

Chan K'in announced that a farewell *bachol* celebration would be conducted in our behalf. It would be observed at the god house, and the gods would be present. Preparations for the bachol fiesta began early on the day before it was held. Mateo would serve as the official host. As such, he

199

would be responsible for the preparation and conduct of the celebration. Four young men were selected to assist him.

Two men went into the jungle and returned with armloads of bark stripped from the sacred bachol tree. They shredded the bark with machetes into small pieces and placed them in the sacred dugout located in front of the god house. A proportionate amount of sugar cane stalks were chopped into bits and added to the bachol bark. The ingredients were beaten with the butt ends of long poles until the juices were extracted, after which the bark and sugar cane pulp residue was removed and discarded. The dugout was covered with fresh banana leaves and the juices left to ferment until the beginning of the fiesta on the next day.

While the two men were making the bachol drink, another man was engaged in gathering a large amount of resin from the sacred copal tree. The copal resin was transformed into small pellets of pom, the incense that would be burned in the god pots.

The final preparations for the celebration were made on the morning of March 21. A large net of handwoven fiber rope was filled with bachol drinking bowls that were hanging from the god house rafters. The bowls were taken to the stream near our hut and given a perfunctory rinsing in

200

the roiled water, and returned to the god house.

Mateo formed a mat of banana leaves immediately in front of the altar board. He placed pom pellets in each of the god pots and ignited them. When the clouds of black and oily smoke billowed to the ceiling, Mateo squatted on his haunches on the mat and began the chant that would summon the gods to come and begin the festivities.

After the gods had presumably arrived, Mateo filled a large clay bowl with water and placed it on the ground in front of the god house. He secured a gourd dipper and a clay bowl and went to the sacred dugout, where he ladled the bowl half full of bachol. On the way back to the god house he stopped and washed his hands in the bowl of water. Proceeding to the front of the altar board, he squatted on the banana leaf mat. With a small ladle formed from a section of banana leaf, he dipped a small quantity of bachol from the serving bowl and trickled the liquid down the throat passage of the center god pot, which represented the chief god Hachak'yum. He repeated the performance until all of the nine gods had received a drink of bachol.

I asked Chan K'in if the gods enjoyed a fiesta. He said the gods were pleased to come to the god house and drink bachol with the Lacandons.

201

"The gods say, 'It is good for men to drink much bachol and be happy.' "

After the gods had been served bachol, it was time for the men to enjoy their share. They washed their hands in the bowl of water, and grouped themselves in two circles inside of the god house. In front of each man a bowl rested on a banana leaf. One of Mateo's assistants filled the bowls with bachol. Jon and I were each given a bowlful. Estelle, who had been standing at the edge of the clearing, was invited by Chan K'in to join the party. She was given a bowl of bachol. The ban on women taking part in a god house activity was lifted in Estelle's case. It indicated the high regard in which she was held by the Lacandons.

Chan K'in started the fiesta by lifting his bowl to his lips. We sat and drank with the men, but declined a refill of our bowls. We did not like the flavor of the bitter bachol bark juice. The sacred dugout contained enough bachol to float it. The Lacandons were determined to drink it dry as quickly as possible.

The bachol was totally consumed by three o'clock in the afternoon. The beverage had left its effect on the men, partially from the minimal alcohol content, but primarily from the quantity consumed. Several men were asleep on the ground in front of the god house. The young man we

202

called Puck had staggered into the jungle to relieve himself. On his return to the god house he had curled up on the trail and fallen asleep.

Chan K'in managed to walk to his hut and eat a number of tortillas before falling into his hammock. We assumed that the bachol celebration was ended. Very late in the day we were astonished to learn that Chan K'in had enjoyed the fiesta so much that he directed a new batch of bachol be brewed immediately. The celebration would be a two-days' affair. Those who were physically able began the preparations, and soon the thumping of poles in the sacred dugout echoed throughout the village.

After our evening meal, Jon departed for a site from which he could observe the setting sun paint its usual colorful masterpiece on the serene waters of the lake. Estelle and I went for a walk on the trail that led to the lake's north side. We stopped on the crest of the high hill overlooking the village to sit on a windfall and catch our breath. From our position we could see the trail below us that we had followed from the village. I looked down the pathway and saw little Ky'um running swiftly up the hill toward us. He was waving his arms and shouting.

Sensing that something quite serious had happened, we left our seat on the windfall and ran to meet Ky'um. There had been an accident at

203

the village. Our prankster, Puck, had slashed himself with a machete, and was bleeding terribly. Ky'um had been dispatched to fetch me. Our whereabouts had not been a problem, for the Lacandons always knew where we were.

Ky'um walked with Estelle, and I ran ahead. I found Puck at the rear of his hut, surrounded by men, women, and children. Most of them were awaiting their turn to affix a loop of string around his left wrist. Puck was sitting on the ground. He was grinning foolishly and staring at the stream of blood pouring from an ugly gash at the base of his thumb. His young wife, Chan Nuk, was crying as she tried to stem the flow of blood.

It developed that Puck, still under the influence of bachol, had tried to cut some firewood for his wife. Holding a piece of wood with his left hand, he had swung his machete. Instead of splitting the wood, he had sliced his thumb. Puck was indeed fortunate that his hand was not severed.

As I was applying pressure to stop the hemorrhaging, Puck's father came near and looked at the wound. He did not tie a string around his son's wrist to ward off the evil dwarfs, but spat on the gashed thumb and walked away, softly chanting to the gods. I stopped the bleeding and cleansed the wound with alcohol, which must have felt like a hot torch application. Puck merely sucked in his breath, and continued his fatuous smiling. I applied a sterile dressing and bandage to the cut, and placed the arm in a sling. I persuaded Puck to swallow two sulfonamide tablets, and directed that he go to bed and remain quiet.

I visited Puck the next morning and redressed the wound. I gave him more sulfonamide tablets and cautioned him to keep the dressing dry and clean, and not to remove it for any reason. The now-sober young man was in good spirits and enjoyed the personal attention I had given him.

The bachol fiesta was renewed in the early afternoon. A man came to our hut and asked Jon and me to come to the god house. We were amazed at what we saw when we arrived. Yesterday's celebration had been mild compared to what was now taking place. The men had dispensed with the bowls they had used the day before. They were now drinking from large gourds of no less than one gallon in capacity. Puck was sitting in the circle of men, as happy as he could be, although somewhat handicapped by the bandaged thumb and his arm in a sling.

Chan K'in greeted us and gave us a bowl of bachol. We stayed until our drink was finished and returned to our hut. A couple of hours later,

205

K'in Bor appeared in the doorway. Chan K'in wanted me to return to the god house, with my harmonica. I found the group sitting in what was now a mere semblance of a circle, glassy-eyed, clutching the gourds of bachol. The laughter and loud conversation that had been predominant earlier had been replaced by yawns and silence.

I played the harmonica and the men nodded their appreciation for my efforts. I was offered more bachol. It did not seem to offend or disturb the Lacandons that I refused to have one more drink with them. When Chan K'in curled up on the floor of the god house, pillowed his head on an arm and closed his eyes, I left the memorable bachol party and rejoined my family.

The twenty-third of March was a quiet day in the village. The men slept most of the day, recuperating from the two successive days of bachol drinking. We also took a holiday from our work schedule, for it was Estelle's birthday. A few weeks earlier, Jon would have presented her with a dozen beautiful orchids that were blooming in the jungle, but the season was now over. He picked and arranged a bouquet of assorted wild flowers, trimmed with lacy fern, and brightened his mother's heart, and our hut. I presented her with a special poem that I had composed for the occasion.

Jon and I had brought a canned Texas pecan

206

cake from the United States, and had kept it secreted among the supplies. We presented the cake to a surprised and delighted Estelle with all of the pomp and ceremony we could muster. As luck would have it, several of our young Lacandon friends walked in as Estelle was cutting her birthday cake. The cake was much too small to share with the wide-eyed and hopeful children. We gave them each a handful of candy, and we ate the cake. Thus, everybody was happy.

The Lacandons do not celebrate or observe birthdays. The women, particularly, have no conception of time. On one occasion Chan K'in left on a visit to a Tzeltal Indian village located a full day's walk to the east of Lake Na'ha. He expected to be away from home for a minimum time of two days. His number one wife, Chan Nuk, worried about Chan K'in's return before the first day had passed. The distraught old woman neglected her work and spent most of the second day watching the trail that would lead her man home.

The day before our departure from Na'ha was hectic. Our hut was the focal point of village activity from sunrise until late evening. Ky'um and his friends were with us constantly. The other people visited us alternately throughout the day, with the men taking the unprecedented action of bringing their wives with them. Many

207

of the callers demonstrated their unspoken feelings with farewell gifts of their handiwork, such as clay likenesses of the jaguar, monkey, tapir, and teposquintl. We also received clay models of Lacandon men, women, and children, all dressed in native attire.

Between the frequent interruptions we managed to pack the things we would take with us. Pepe Martinez had given us the passenger and cargo weight limitation of his airplane, but without verifying scales we could only estimate the total weight of our cargo. We discovered that many items would have to be left behind. Except for the next morning's breakfast needs, we gave each Lacandon family a share of the remaining food stocks. Estelle gathered the pots, pans, plates, and many aluminum kitchen utensils and distributed them among the families, giving priority to the young married couples. Mosquito netting, lengths of rope, the cargo bags, and other items were given to the men. The children fell heir to the nearly depleted supplies of cookies and candy.

The attendance at the last evening session at our hut grew until there was no room for more. The usual horseplay, laughter, and high spirits were notably missing. Conversation was held to a bare minimum. Occasionally one would leave, to return later, or to be replaced by another. At

208

twilight an eight-year-old lad came to our hut. He shyly approached Estelle and gave her a small bouquet of exquisite, fusia-colored flowers. In a soft voice the boy said, *"Bini'kat'en!"* (*"Good-bye!"*), and ran swiftly from the hut. The warmth and absolute sincerity of the unspoiled child of nature, and his simple token of love, overwhelmed us. Sometimes, the tears rise easily.

Of all the Lacandons, little Ky'um was the most visibly affected by our pending departure. He followed Jon's every move, and as the day went by he became more depressed and uncommunicative. By the end of the day the poor boy was so emotionally upset that he went to his home and to bed. Our deep-felt concern for our beloved Ky'um caused us a long and restless night.

The morning of March 27 eventually dawned. Our first visitor was Ky'um. He bounced into the hut wearing his usual captivating smile, and gave us five fresh eggs. We had completed our rather skimpy breakfast, but there was a pan of water still on the fire. We hard-boiled the eggs and ate them on the spot.

Chan K'in was our next caller. My generous friend was bearing a gift for me — another bundle of cured tobacco leaves. I tried to tell him that I was unable to take the tobacco with me for lack of stowing space, but the old fellow insisted that I take it. I did not want to seem unkind, so I agreed to accept the tobacco.

K'in Bor, who was Estelle's favorite of the young men, brought her a farewell offering of a sprig of vanilla beans that he had gone to the jungles and found that morning. We enjoyed the subtle fragrance of the vanilla beans for weeks afterward.

While Jon and I tidied up the hut, Estelle toured the village and said final good-byes to the women and girls. She paused at Chan K'in's hut and gave the girl with the badly scarred face a tube of lipstick and a bottle of bright red nail polish. The girl was so pleased and excited she nearly cried.

Before we left the village I once again examined Puck's injured thumb, which I had done every day since his accident. When I told him that the wound was healed to the point where a dressing was no longer necessary, Puck looked so disappointed that I soothed him with a farewell bandage.

Ky'um and K'in Bor helped carry our packs to a dugout and then paddled us across the lake to the north side. One man remained in the village, and all of the other men and the older boys had taken the trail and were waiting at the edge of the airstrip when we arrived.

The plane was late in arriving, but we did

210

not mind. We enjoyed the extra time we had with our friends. We were sitting on the ground talking when Ky'um held up a hand for silence. He listened intently for a moment, and announced, "Pepe is coming!" His fellows all agreed, and rose to their feet. We did not hear the drone of the approaching aircraft until a full three minutes after Ky'um's warning.

While Pepe loaded our possessions aboard the plane, we shook hands with each of the Lacandons. Jon and Ky'um found it difficult to say good-bye to each other. In a final gesture of farewell, Chan K'in placed an arm around my shoulders and said, "You are a very good friend. You will come back?" I pressed his gnarled hands in mine and assured him that we would plan to return some day.

As the plane circled Lake Na'ha after takeoff we passed over the village. Far below us, women and children stood apart from the thatched huts and waved their arms as we flew out of their lives, but surely not out of their hearts.

The hardships and discomforts we had undergone in the dangerous and unhealthy environment of the Selva Lacandon would soon be forgotten. But we shall never forget the beautiful people of Na'ha. They had graciously permitted us to learn much about their ancient and primitive life-style. Beyond that, and of greater impor-

211

APPENDIX

Phonetic Glossary of Maya words and terms used by the Lacandon, with English equivalents:

Maya	English
AA'CH	Baby
A'ACK'SA'KIN	Venus (star)
AG'BE	"Goodnight"
AK'BIR	Night
AK'NA	Moon
AK'NOK	Men's clothing
AK'UN	River
AK'YUM	Gods
A'YIM	Alligator
B'AK	Meat

Maya	English
BA'K	Animal
BAK'ER	Body
BA'ROOM	Jaguar
BE'H	Trail (pathway)
BINI'KAT'EN	"Good-bye"
B'OOR	Beans
BO'SH	Banana
BUH	Owl
BU'HEK	"Hello"
CHAC	Rain
CHAK'UR'KIN	Hot
CHE'	Stick of wood
CHEE'CH	Birds
CHEE'NA	Orange
CHEM	Dugout canoe
CHI'	Mouth
CHI'BA'KAN	Snakebite
CHO	Rat
CHUH	Gourd

Maya	English
CHUR	Flute
CHU'RUK	Bow
CO'H	Teeth
GUN'EN	Sleep
HA'	Water (also "rain")
HACH'A'NOK	Women's clothing
HAN'AN	Eat
HAR'AR	Arrow
HOTZ'KA	"Good morning"
K'AI	Fish
K'AK	Fire
K'AN	Snake, sky
K'ASH	Chicken
K'AY	Sing
K'IK	Sister (same for brother)
K'IN	Sun, day
KIN'SAH	Kill
KUCH'E	Cedar
KUCHE'ROO	Knife

215

Maya	English
KUK'AY	Music
KUK'HAHAP'KUH	Lightning
K'UM	Squash (vegetable)
K'UP	Hands
KY'SIN	Storm
K'YUM	Drum
LA'K	Wife (same for husband)
LUM	Ground
MA'OOTS	Sickness
MA'SA	Monkey
MASK'A	Machete
ME'HEN'PA	Children
ME'HE'PA	Boy, or girl
MILPA (Aztec origin)	Cornfield
MU'YAR	Clouds
NA'	Mother
NA'CHI'SUR	Foreigner (man who can read or write)

216

Maya	English
NET'SOY ENG'WOR	To be happy
NI'	Nose
NO'KOR	Worm
N'TEK	Father
NU'KU'CHI	Tree
N'UR	Corn
OCH'I	Food
OKO'CA'KIN	"Good afternoon"
OO'BAR'KAN	Stars
OOK	Feet
OO'S	Mosquito, gnat, fly
OO'YAK'AK'U	God house
PA'IK	Plant (sow)
PE'K	Dog
PET'HA	Lake
PO'	Wash
POM	Sacred incense
SAH'Y	Mountain

Maya	English
SHIM'BAR	Hunt
SHI'NAR	Man
SHUP'RAR	Woman
SIK	Bat (mammal)
SIN'IK	Ant
SIS	Cold
SOT	Rattle
SOT'SA'HOR	Hair
SUK IN WIN'IK	"My friend"
TAR'A	Touch
TI'AR	Son, or daughter
TOK'IK	Burn
TO'ROK	Lizard
T'SIK	Angry
T'SI'MIN	Horse
TUK'UR	Sad
TU'NICH	Rock, or stone
TU'NU	Snail
U'PEK KY'SIN	Earthquake

Maya	English
UT'SAY'IR	Birth
WAH	Tortilla
WA'YAK	Dream
WIK'IN	Death, or to die
YAK'OSH	Eggs
YUK	Deer